Apr 11   '67

PORTRAIT OF AN IRISHMAN

T. W. ROLLESTON

PORTRAIT OF AN IRISHMAN

A Biographical Sketch of
T. W. ROLLESTON

by
COMMANDER C. H. ROLLESTON
R.N. (RETIRED)

FOREWORD BY
STEPHEN GWYNN

14 PLATES

METHUEN & CO. LTD. LONDON
36 Essex Street, Strand, W.C.2

First published in 1939

PRINTED IN GREAT BRITAIN

TO

R. B.

AS A TOKEN OF A VERY SINCERE AFFECTION AND
IN MEMORY OF SOME OF THE STORMY SEAS—
AND CALM WATERS TOO—WE HAVE NAVIGATED
TOGETHER

FOREWORD

THIS book throws much light on the beginnings of the Irish literary movement in which T. W. Rolleston was a distinguished and most decorative figure.

The movement was a side-shoot of the Irish Revolution which began when I was a schoolboy and even now is hardly complete. But Ireland which sixty years ago was governed by landlords under the British parliament is now entirely self-governing and the landlord power has ceased to exist. Moreover, sixty years ago there was very little literature in the English tongue that could be properly called Irish ; to-day there is a great body of Irish work known wherever English is read, and Rolleston contributed powerfully to its creation. His importance was rather as an organising and inspiring personality than as an actual creator ; but at least one poem of his will always find a place in every anthology of Irish poetry.

His son's book tells the story, largely through extracts from his early speeches and writings ; all that I need do is to set down some personal impressions of the man.

We were at the same school, St. Columba's, but as he was seven years my elder I never knew him there except as a distinguished ' old boy ' remarkable for his personal beauty. His University was Dublin, and I went to Oxford. But when my father came up to take charge of the Divinity School in T.C.D. I saw as much of Trinity as I did of Brasenose ; for my father had a genius for making friends with young men and Rolleston was the first in a long series of favourites who became familiar in our house. He was indeed a cousin not more than four or five times removed (which among us is not a distant relationship), but the real tie was literature and he was constantly seen about in my father's company—with one comic result. Rolleston was also devoted to the society of John O'Leary, the ex-Fenian, then restored to Ireland after long exile in Paris. O'Leary was a lean eagle-beaked old man, but the same description would have applied perfectly to my father, and when John Yeats exhibited a portrait of O'Leary at the Hibernian Academy many visitors took it for a portrait of the Professor of Divinity. Finally Rolleston brought about a meeting. 'Well, now, Dr. Gwynn,' said O'Leary with the elaborate courtesy that always marked him, 'in view of this resemblance that is said to exist between us, all I can say is I hope that neither of us will say or do anything that will in any way compromise the other.'

My father, it should be observed, was a good Unionist but that did not lessen his sympathy for Rolleston, who was, like O'Leary, an aristocratic Nationalist. The men of the Fenian period, and still more the survivors from 1848, incline to regard the Land War as a vulgar quarrel about rents. Rolleston, I think, shared this feeling. It was generally understood that he and other leading spirits of the Dublin intelligentsia would have been welcomed in Parnell's party but that they were unwilling to be bound by the party pledge. At all events Rolleston, then and thereafter, avoided identifying himself with the popular movement while Yeats, equally disdainful of mere politicians, joined the secret Irish Republican Brotherhood.

Literature was an open field and Rolleston from the first not only hoped for a revival of interest in Irish hero stories, but was confident that Yeats was the poet to revive them. He helped perhaps more than any one else to create an atmosphere which fostered the development of Yeats's genius, and helped to prevent it from losing itself in a vague mysticism. Edward Dowden, then Professor of English Literature in Trinity, was of great value to the younger men. He was himself strongly opposed to Irish nationalism, but he had a genial interest in all literary activities and his house in Temple Road was a great meeting-place on Sunday afternoons. Rolleston had been one of his most brilliant pupils and in many ways resembled him—especially in appreciation of the German genius and of Walt Whitman. Douglas Hyde, already preaching revival of the Gaelic language, was a constant figure at these gatherings, and so was Yeats as well as his delightful father the painter. Looking back now it seems to me that most of the young men who gathered about Dowden's bland and richly cultivated intelligence were in one way or another supporters of a general Irish movement which he most fiercely opposed.

The break-up of Parnell's leadership shattered and scattered much in Ireland, and during the nineties party politics were repellent even to men less fastidious than Rolleston. Horace Plunkett's arrival on the Irish scene offered a new and more attractive leadership, and there was a special charm for literary men in his genuine admiration for anybody who could write. He had a profound belief in the value of literary intelligence for the work of economic propaganda, and Rolleston, whose mind was admirably adaptable, was the very man to assist him. How much Plunkett and his associates actually achieved for the betterment of Ireland, it would be hard to say ; still harder to distinguish how far Rolleston contributed to the result. One who is by nature an organiser and assistant, who is content to take his part in team work, earns no distinctive recognition ; and that was Rolleston's way whether in literature or in economics. The best of him went into a general impersonal achievement; even his writings are for the most part work of popularisation. But, as happens to a few men among the writers of each generation, once at least he produced a little masterpiece. ' The Dead at Clonmacnois ' is in the tradition of Ferguson, but Ferguson never did anything so completely good. Apart from this, I should put Rolleston's verses on his Rob Roy canoe, and those on his bicycle, above the rest of his work, scholarly and accomplished though it was. They convey more of the man's personality.

On the Irish question generally, many of the views expressed in this book, by him or by his son, are singularly unlike my own. I was an Irish Nationalist who worked with the Irish Party over a long period of years and was proud of my leaders. But I worked also closely with Horace Plunkett during the Irish Convention of 1917 and should like to add this word. Rolleston did not live to see self-government established in Ireland ; Plunkett and I did. Neither of us had any cause to love the process by which it came to pass ; for that matter, his house and mine were destroyed in the same week by Irish Nationalists. But after self-government had been a few years at work, creating order out of the chaos which had been handed over, I saw with pleasure a letter from Plunkett declaring that the Irish Free State had produced in Patrick Hogan

the best Minister of Agriculture in Europe.   If Rolleston were
alive to-day I think he would have modified a good many of
his views.   I am sure that he would have been not less but
more constant in his Irish Nationalism.

STEPHEN GWYNN

DUBLIN, 1939

PREFACE

IN putting together this outline of my father's life and work I have been mindful of the fact that a son is naturally inclined to be biased in his father's favour and open therefore to the charge of having over-stressed the significance of his actions, sayings, and writings.

As my only desire is to be strictly accurate I have therefore allowed my father to speak for himself wherever possible. Fortunately this could be done because, although he seems to have destroyed all his diaries except those for 1897 and 1912–15, copies have been preserved of his more important articles, speeches, and pamphlets. These contain in perhaps a more convenient form what might otherwise have been found in his diary.

Opinions of his work and of the man himself held by others outside his own family circle are also available and I have drawn on them freely when it has appeared that an opinion independent of my own was required.

I have not attempted to adhere to any chronological sequence; this would have been possible in the case of a man whose whole life had been spent in one sphere of activity, e.g. diplomacy, politics, journalism, the stage, and so on ; but in my father's case any attempt to deal with his life from year to year would have involved alluding to perhaps a dozen different subjects in each section of the book and reverting to all of them in the next section, besides introducing new subjects. The story of his connection with any one activity would therefore have been scattered through the book and the result would have been a confused and disconnected patchwork.

For this reason I have tried to deal with each phase of his life separately and to finish with it before going back in years and starting on another.

I know this is an unusual way in which to write a ' life ', but then my father was an unusual man.

I hope the result may not be entirely without interest.

C. H. ROLLESTON

HAMPSTEAD, N.W.3, 1939

ACKNOWLEDGMENTS

I WISH to express my grateful thanks to the Publishing Houses and the Proprietors of the publications listed below for permission, where this has been obtainable, to reproduce the various and considerable extracts from books, pamphlets, addresses, speeches, and letters which appear herein.

I have endeavoured to get in touch with everybody concerned, but in some cases it would appear that the firm or publication involved has either gone out of business or ceased publication. If for this reason any one has been overlooked, I hope those concerned will accept this expression of thanks for consents which I feel sure would have been given.

The Times, the *Nineteenth Century and After*, the *Observer*, the *Irish Weekly Independent*, the *Irish Times*, the *Daily Telegraph and Morning Post*, the *Derry Journal*, the *Irish Church Quarterly*, the *Irish Booklover*, the *North American Review*. A. D. Innes & Co., Ltd., George G. Harrap & Co., John Murray, Constable & Co., The Talbot Press, George Allen & Unwin, Ltd., Maunsel and Co., Ltd., M. H. Gill and Son, Smith Elder & Co., Ltd., Elkin Mathews & Marrot, Ltd., Hodges, Figgis & Co., Ltd., William Heinemann, Ltd., John Lane, The Bodley Head, Ltd., and Ivor Nicholson & Watson, Ltd.

CONTENTS

ILLUSTRATIONS

I

INTRODUCTION

IT is almost, if not quite, impossible to read any book about Ireland and Irish affairs or any Irish biography or volume of recollections published within the last forty or fifty years without coming across references to T. W. Rolleston. If any one cared to extract these allusions to a very remarkable man he would be forced to the conclusion that ' T. W. R.' had made an impression in many different spheres of activity ; which would be no less than strictly true. He was Head of his Public School, St. Columba's College, Rathfarnham, County Dublin ; he had a very distinguished career at Trinity College, where he won the Vice-Chancellor's Prize for English Verse and was a contemporary of Oscar Wilde. As a German scholar and an authority on German literature and philosophy he was probably head and shoulders ahead of any of his contemporaries and in fact at the close of his life he had been for many years in charge of the German section of *The Times Literary Supplement*. He was a co-founder with Ernest Rhys and William Butler Yeats of the famous Rhymers' Club of the early nineties which held its meetings at the Cheshire Cheese. He helped to start, and was the first Managing Director of, the Irish Industries Association, where one of his colleagues was his life-long friend, George W. Russell, better known to millions of the lovers of his poetry and other writings as ' AE '. He gave valuable assistance to another intimate friend, Sir Horace Plunkett, in the inception and management of the Irish Agricultural Organisation Society, and when Plunkett was appointed Vice-President of the Department of Agriculture and Technical Instruction for Ireland T. W. R. went with him as Organiser of Lectures. He was the principal founder of the India Society of London which, among other things, made the writings of Sir Rabindranath Tagore so well known in philosophical circles. He was the virtual founder

I

of the Irish Literary Society of London, many of the early meetings for the formation of which were held at his house, ' Birnam ', 10 Spencer Hill, Wimbledon ; he was the first Honorary Secretary of the Society. He organised and took charge of the Irish Historic Loan Collection at the St. Louis Exhibition of 1904. He was Librarian of the Department— afterwards the Ministry—of Information during the war and made use also of his intricate knowledge of the Irish and other languages in the Obscure Languages Section of the Censor's Department. He was a member of the Old Boys Corps and later of the Inns of Court Volunteers and spent several nights per week at the age of sixty on the roof of a city building waiting to repel German Air Raids with a machine-gun.

In between he found time to be a keen botanist and biologist, to go for long voyages in a Rob Roy canoe made by himself, to do an immense amount of bicycling, to be an amateur actor, to take a more than passing interest in psychical pheno- mena, to be a poet of distinction, to be Taylorian Lecturer at Oxford, to contribute frequent articles to the *Nineteenth Century*, which he edited for a short period, and many other journals, to be leader writer on the Dublin *Daily Express* and Irish correspondent of the London *Daily Chronicle*, and to bring up two families. He was married twice : first to Edith de Burgh, of Kildare, who died in 1896, and second—in 1897—to Maud, one of the six daughters of the Rev. Stopford Brooke, the famous preacher, poet, and literateur.

As befits a man who had such a distinguished career T. W. R. had a distinguished ancestry. The Rolleston family is one of the oldest in the Kingdom ; when others aver that they ' came over with the Conqueror ' we are able to reply that we were already in England before him and are actually of his family, being descended from that Rolfe the Northman, or Rollo the Dane as he is sometimes called, who settled in Staffordshire in the tenth century, and seized that part of Northern France which then became Normandy or ' The Northland '. The village of Rolleston-on-Dove,[1] a few miles from Burton-on- Trent, was originally ' Rolvesdun ' or ' Rollo's Town '.

A brief history of the family is given on the pedigree which is preserved at ffranckfort Castle, the headquarters of the Irish Rollestons near the village of Dunkerrin almost on the

---

[1] Rhymes with ' cove ' not ' love '.

APPROACH TO ROLLESTON FROM BURTON-ON-TRENT

ROLLESTON'S FATHER AND MOTHER, CHARLES ROLLESTON-SPUNNER, Q.C., AND HIS WIFE, ELIZABETH, DAUGHTER OF BARON RICHARDS, AT THE TIME OF THEIR MARRIAGE ABOUT 1832

border of Tipperary and King's County. The following is an extract therefrom :

> The Rev. Richard, John, and Arthur Rolleston came to Ireland in the year 1610, they having received from King James I by Patent dated at Westminster the 10th day of May, 1610, a large grant of land in the County of Armagh, namely in the Barony of Onelan, Parish of Kilmore, the Townland of Agheovery alias Carnecapull, and in the Parish of Mullagh-bracke the Manor of Teemore (Tymore) containing 8½ Townlands, with proviso that the said Richard Rolleston should not let or sell any part of the same grant to any Irishman or other person who had not taken the Oath of Supremacy before the Lord Chancellor six months before or after such demise. Richard and his brother-in-law in 1618 let all these premises to Sir Francis Annesley, afterwards Lord Mountnorris, and to Sir John Boucher, and to others who had not taken the required oath, and upon this inquisition Lord Mountnorris takes possession of the property, namely the Manor of Tymore. In the year 1637 the Earl of Strafford reinstated the heir of Richard Rolleston on petition and this matter forms the sixth article of Impeachment against Lord Strafford, on whose fall Lord Mountnorris regained possession.

In 1670 an attempt, which was not successful, was made to recover these lands, and the history goes on to state that the descendants of Arthur Rolleston represent the senior branch of the family, now settled at ffranckfort Castle.

So much for the family history. At the present time the head of the family is James Rolleston, my second cousin, of ffranckfort Castle, and the English branch of the family is distinguished by such men as Sir Lancelot Rolleston, of Watnall Hall, Nottinghamshire, and Sir Humphry Rolleston, Bart., the celebrated physician.

ffranckfort Castle is a lovely old place, built by O'Malley, King of Ormonde in the twelfth century and therefore probably the oldest structure of its kind which is still in use as a residence. It is surrounded by a moat and had the usual drawbridge and portcullis leading through a high stone wall into the Castle grounds.

There is a sundial in the grounds which interested my father sufficiently to induce him to write about it to his friend, Dr. Douglas Hyde, now President of Eire, in August 1897 :

DEAR HYDE,
I found these verses on a sundial at ffranckfort Castle, King's County, the house of my cousin, Major Charles Rolleston.
Sundial was made some twenty years ago by a man of

mechanical turn, then a pauper in Roscrea Workhouse. I understand he composed the verses too.

> Ladies and gentlemen, this is my plan
> To view the pace of yonder sun ;
> And count the hours upon my fan,
> The daily race he has to run.

Yours ever,
T. W. R.

Thomas William Rolleston was born about five miles from ffranckfort Castle at Glasshouse, near the village of Shinrone, seven miles from Roscrea. His father was Charles Rolleston-Spunner, Q.C., who adopted the additional name on inheriting an estate in 1867 from Thomas Spunner, J.P. This, however, was ten years after my father was born, the youngest of three sons, and neither he nor either of his elder brothers was obliged to add the surname of Spunner. The eldest brother, Charles James, went into the Indian Army but retired as a Captain and thereafter lived a rather lonely life in London, interesting himself mainly in Indian affairs and writing a little now and then. He published one book, *The Age of Folly*, in 1911 and was engaged for many years in collecting information for another to be called ' Lost Secrets ', but this was never completed, though the manuscript has been preserved.

The second brother, Henry Barry, farmed the Glasshouse property very successfully and married his first cousin, Ida Richards.

My father also had one sister, Catherine, who married Henry Truell, of Clonmannon, County Wicklow, but she died in 1890 at a comparatively early age, much to my father's sorrow as they had been a particularly devoted brother and sister. Henry Truell made a fortune in the Klondyke gold rush and left most of it to Dr. Barnardo's Homes, where his name is perpetuated by a plate over one of the beds known as the ' Truell Bed '.

My grandmother, the mother of these four children, was Elizabeth, daughter of a famous Irish Judge, the Right Honourable John Richards, a Baron of the Court of Exchequer, Ireland.

Charles Rolleston-Spunner, Q.C., afterwards County Court Judge of Tipperary, was one of the best known men of his time. Very handsome, witty, and kind he was a famous and much sought-after pleader at the bar, and when he became a Judge his Courts were renowned not only for the fairness with which the law was administered but for the sense of humanity which he brought to bear on every matter that came before him. A brilliant barrister, a brilliant Judge, and one of the best-liked men in Ireland, when my grandfather married the beautiful and almost equally gifted daughter of Baron Richards, they were possibly the most distinguished-looking and most popular young couple in Irish society.

It is from them that T. W. Rolleston inherited his own brilliant gifts and his mother's strong personality. As far as she was concerned there was never any question as to who was mistress in her house, and in later years she can only be described as a domestic autocrat of the old-fashioned kind ; there were in fact occasional conflicts with her eldest sons and with her two daughters-in-law. She had a horror of insects and for that reason would not tolerate flowers in the house, lest a spider or a caterpillar might be lurking among the leaves or blossoms. My grandmother even carried this antipathy as far as to throw out of the window flowers that her sons' wives might have brought in to decorate their rooms. She played the harp exquisitely.

My father's early life as the son of parents of such outstanding distinction was also undoubtedly influenced by the fact that his two brothers were seventeen and twenty years older than himself. My grandfather was born in 1807 and was married in about 1835 ; two sons and a daughter were born within the next few years, but he was fifty years of age, before T. W. Rolleston made his entry into the world in 1857. My father was therefore the son of parents who were at least middle-aged when he was born and his early life became in consequence almost that of an only child ; those who surrounded him were all grown-up and of the four children he was unquestionably the favourite. He was too, if not exactly a precocious child, at least possessed of intelligence far in advance of the normal for his years. I have heard it said that he was interested in the *Pickwick Papers* at the age of one, but I fancy this must be an exaggeration.

Not having any brothers and sisters of his own age he was

compelled to rely largely on himself for amusement and occupation at a period when, in any case, families and communities had to be far more self-contained where such matters were concerned than is necessary to-day. There were no motor-cars, no cinemas, no wireless, and a visit to neighbours was something of an expedition. This made my father self-reliant to a degree and also somewhat reserved, a quality he never entirely lost even where his own children were later on concerned. We seldom knew what he was doing or thinking and were disinclined to enquire as to what might be interesting him at any moment. This attitude of reserve, which kept us always a little in awe of him, was undoubtedly a legacy from the comparative loneliness of his early years, at least where companions of his own age were concerned.

Not much is known about his school life nor of his life at Trinity College, but it is easy to deduce that he must have stood rather apart, both humanly and intellectually, from his schoolmates and College contemporaries ; he played games, especially Rugby football, well if not brilliantly, and was the only person who had ever jumped a horse over the sunk fence between the garden and the back lawn at Glasshouse.

Glasshouse, where he spent his early life and which we, his children, remember as the place where we went for many happy holidays is, alas, no more. The house was built on the site of an ancient glass factory and on my Uncle Henry's death in 1910 his widow sold the property and after various other changes of ownership, due it has been said to its over-population with ghosts, it was finally purchased by the Monks of a large Trappist Monastery not far from Roscrea. They pulled the house down and used the stone for extensions to the Monastery. It had been a grand old house, built in Cromwellian times, and had among other attractions an avenue of beech trees—green and copper—which must have been almost unrivalled, certainly in Ireland.

T. W. Rolleston had eight children, three sons and one daughter of his first marriage, and two sons and two daughters of the second. The eldest of these, Hugh Charles, would possibly have followed in his father's literary footsteps had circumstances been different. He was not physically strong, however, and, after service in the Australian Expeditionary Force during the war, he died in Brisbane in 1921. Arthur

ROLLESTON AT 19

FRANCKFORT CASTLE

GLASSHOUSE

George, who came next, passed out of Woolwich as Senior Gunner of his batch, joined the Field Artillery, got his jacket, served throughout the war in France and Italy, and is now Brigadier, R.A., Scottish Command. He married in 1916 the Hon. Susan Butler-Massey, daughter of Baron Clarina of Elm Park, Limerick, and has two sons.

My sister, Una Gwynn, whose second name marks our relationship to the famous Irish Gwynn family of whom Stephen is probably the best known, married in 1912, Bronson Albery, one of the three sons of Mary Moore (Mrs. James Albery) the famous actress, who afterwards married Sir Charles Wyndham. Bronson is Managing Director of the family theatres built or acquired by Sir Charles and Lady Wyndham—the ' New ', ' Criterion ', and ' Wyndham's '. They have two sons and two daughters.

I was the youngest of the first family and after me came Owen Molony, Honor Stopford, Patrick William, and Aideen Maud in that order. Honor is the wife of William Dockar Drysdale and Aideen is married to George A. Riding, M.A., Head Master of Aldenham School, Elstree, Herts.

It might be said of my father that a man who dabbled in so many different things as are comprised in the summary of his activities already given, and who in addition found time for a large amount of original writing, would not be likely to achieve distinction in any particular sphere. Though in the case of another man this would very probably be a fair conclusion it was certainly not correct where T. W. R. was concerned. For one thing he did not ' dabble ' ; whatever he did, he did with all his might, with an almost unbelievable enthusiasm, and with a thoroughness that amazed all who came into contact with him. Perhaps when he slept his brain ceased to work, but it never did so at other times ; if he was not actually working at his desk in an office or in his study at home he was thinking out the best method of attacking whatever problem was uppermost at the moment. He had the faculty too of working and thinking in spite of distractions that would have diverted the attention of any ordinary indi-vidual. On one occasion, for example, a young lady who sat beside him in a Dublin tram carried on with him for twenty minutes or so a conversation of the sort that one does perhaps

carry on in a tram. The car stopped outside our house—
we were living then at 104 Pembroke Road—and father got
out. As he was putting his latchkey in the door he noticed
that the young lady had followed him ; he turned round to
speak to her only to find that he had been carrying on a
conversation with his own daughter without knowing in the
least who she was ! Perhaps a hundredth part of his brain
had been talking to Una while the other ninety-nine parts were
working on an article or trying to solve the insoluble Irish
problem.

On another occasion, when Rolleston was crossing the
Atlantic on his way to the St. Louis Exhibition of 1904, he
had gone on deck for some air and exercise, leaving for the
moment some last-minute work in connection with the Irish
Historic Loan Collection which was to be displayed in the
' Irish Village ' at St. Louis. Leaning against the rail and
looking down on the swirling water close to the ship's side he
was struck by the variegated, ever-changing, and vari-coloured
pattern woven by the ship's passage through the water. There
were lines and splashes of every shade of blue and green,
with here and there a streak of foam and an occasional wavelet
as the ship rolled slightly. Rolleston set his brain to work
and in a few moments he had sketched a design for a rug
which should catch and imprison the pattern on the water.
On his return to Ireland he had the rug made at one of the
centres of Irish industry which he did so much to foster. It
now lies on the floor of my stepmother's drawing-room in
London.

Rolleston never took up anything without making of it as
thoroughly good a job as was possible, and the total time he
wasted during his life could probably be compressed into
twenty-four hours. He was no dilettante, whatever the matter
in hand, and never left or abandoned any activity till he had
given it all that was in him to give. He neither desired nor
tried to get anything out of it for himself.

One specially Irish characteristic of this apparently tireless
man was, not exactly a contempt for money—of which he had
little enough—but a failure to exact adequate payment for
his work. He helped many others with all his heart and soul
and brain on the road to fame and often to fortune, but
marketed his own services and work for pittances that may have

paid for paper and ink. Had he been gifted with the financial acumen of some of his literary contemporaries—Bernard Shaw and George Moore for example—he might have become a comparatively wealthy man ; as it was, if a publisher offered him £50 for a year's work and the benefit of a lifetime's study he accepted it with gratitude and did the work for its own sake. On one occasion a publisher, having made such a bargain, sent him a cheque for a further £50 shortly after the book had appeared. Rolleston was almost overcome by this act of generosity.

As against this it must be admitted that T. W. R. did not try to write for a ' popular ' market. On one occasion he did publish a lurid short story in the *Pall Mall Magazine* and was paid twelve guineas for it, the Editor having offered twenty guineas if it could be published under the author's own name. Rolleston, however, would have none of it ; he took the smaller sum and the tale appeared as by ' T. W. Rowlandson '. ' Lurid ', by the way, is the right word, seeing that the story concerned an entomologist who descended the crater of a South American volcano in pursuit of a rare butterfly. The volcano elected to erupt and the butterfly-hunter was hard put to it to beat the molten lava to the crater's edge and safety. Cyrus Cuneo illustrated the tale with some graphic drawings.

However, Milton sold *Paradise Lost* for £5 and John Cabot received only twice that amount for crossing the Atlantic in an open boat and discovering Newfoundland, so, judged by those standards, Rolleston can have had no cause for complaint. Complain he certainly never did.

I

LITERARY

THE organisation with which Rolleston was connected and which will be longest remembered was undoubtedly the Irish Literary Society of London. This was an association of Irish writers which came into existence for the purpose of gathering together the numerous loose ends of Irish writings— the straws which were already showing the direction of the wind which, supported by the Irish Literary Society, was to attain the dimensions of a literary gale which has by no means yet blown itself out.

The Irish Literary Society of London was founded in 1893 mainly, it would seem, because T. W. Rolleston was then living in that city. In the same year he had been associated with Sir Charles Gavan Duffy in the formation of a company whose object was to publish and circulate Irish literature. Sir Charles was Chairman of this company, and Rolleston Secretary ; Edmund Downey, the publisher, was also connected with it, and one of the patrons was that grand old Fenian, John O'Leary. This enterprise, though actually founded, came to nothing, but, as Downey subsequently wrote, ' It would not perhaps be fair to say who was to blame for the collapse, but it was certainly not either T. W. Rolleston or I '.

Whether or not this abortive venture led into the Irish Literary Society it is not possible to say ; it may be so, because the first meetings from which that organisation emerged were held alternately in Edmund Downey's house at Clapham and our home in Wimbledon. Gavan Duffy became President of the Society and an interesting sidelight on the whirligig of Irish affairs which had brought Sir Charles and my father into such close contact is afforded by a reminiscence of Downey's. ' I remember on one occasion,' he wrote, ' breakfasting in London with Sir Charles Gavan Duffy and Rolleston ; after some discussion about the " union

of hearts " (which was all the rage at that time) Sir Charles
said, " Well, it is significant at any rate to find me drinking
tea at the same table with the grandson of the Judge who tried
me for high treason." ' The Judge in question was, of course,
Baron Richards, my great-grandfather, Duffy having been
one of the leaders of the rising of 1848. Actually he was
acquitted in the House of Lords on a point of law, and later
went to Australia, where his services were rewarded with a
K.C.M.G., and his son became a very much respected Judge
of the Supreme Court.

Notwithstanding this connection Rolleston and Gavan Duffy
became and remained the greatest of friends ; in the Irish
Literary Society they found a strong common interest, and
Irish men and women with literary inclinations found a source
of encouragement without which the world's literature would
be very much poorer.

Rolleston was the first Honorary Secretary of the Society
which, spurred on by his energy, enthusiasm, and criticism,
led to and became the focus of the Irish Literary movement.
I have been very fortunate in finding in an old book of newspaper cuttings a verbatim report of an address given by him
to the Press Club in Dublin three years after the foundation
of the Society. Much of this address is of great interest to-day
when the Irish language, in spite of Rolleston's doubts, has
actually been revived, though on an artificial foundation,
and when W. B. Yeats, to whom he refers so enthusiastically,
is recognized as probably the greatest poet of the nineteenth
and twentieth centuries who used the English language as his
medium. In 1896, though his work was gaining recognition,
fame was still in the lap of those Irish gods for whom William
Butler Yeats held it in trust till his death in 1939. The cutting
in question is from the *Irish Weekly Independent*, and sets out
much better than any words of mine could do it the aims and
aspirations of the I.L.S.

It is generally admitted [Rolleston said] both by the friends and foes of
the Irish Literary movement—for it has both—that something of the kind
does actually exist ; that we have, in the literal sense, a movement of life
and energy going on in this sphere of Irish life. The movement may be
great or small, but it is worth examination, for no one can say what it
may come to. I suppose most of us here are desirous that it should come
to something, and look with satisfaction on the idea of Ireland's possessing

a powerful and characteristic national literature. Let us consider a little the grounds for this feeling. Let us ask ourselves, in the first place, what literature really is, and in the second what we expect it to do for us. What is literature, to begin with? To take examples, every one will agree that grammars or spelling-books are not 'literature'. Nor is a medical treatise usually considered 'literature'. One might go as far as to say that works of science are not literature; but when we remember the scientific work produced by men like Hugh Millar in the last generation, and Huxley and Tyndall in this, we pause before committing ourselves to such a statement. There is evidently something in the writings of men like these which places their work in a different class from most works of scientific research. What is this difference? What is there in one which is not in the other? If we answer this question we shall be close upon having a good working definition of our subject.

Well, the answer I would suggest is this: We find that some writers, whatever their subject may be, contrive to convey to us a sense of their own personalities in a way which others do not. We feel this personality, this temperament of the individual writer, in a variety of ways—in the selection of the facts with which he deals, in the angle of view from which he looks at them, and in the manner in which he endeavours to make us see them too. In one word, whether literature records facts or fictions, whether it records them in prose or in verse, it always records them as seen through a certain medium—the medium of the writer's own temperament and feeling—while the writing that is not literature records them simply as a photographic plate records, without selection, without favour, without interest or feeling.

Literature, then, is the revelation of a human personality, or of nature reflected in that personality; and the literature of a nation is a revelation of that nation's individual character and temper. Observe now how great and indispensable a part is played by literature in a nation's life. The wisest man among the ancient Greeks used to say that no utterance of human or divine wisdom was greater than that saying of the god of Delphi, 'Know thyself'. Well, it is by literature that a nation learns to know itself. There, as in a magic mirror, it recognises its own features, but it sees them idealised and ennobled, for it sees them reflected in the mind of the poet or the thinker. In that mirror not only the surface of things is reflected, but things invisible to the common eye. There the great events of history are displayed and their significance made clear. And there too we can read with new wonder and delight the story of our common everyday lives—the little successes and defeats that come to every man; the temptations and trials, the loves and sorrows, the silent victories of honour, the tragedies of worldly failures and disaster, and the more pitiful tragedies of the soul's degradation. And there the natural features of the country and the scenes we witness every hour are made to impress themselves on our imaginations as they never would if we did not see them through eyes more gifted than our own. The sunset burns with a richer and more mysterious light; the mountains rise with greater majesty; the woods and fields are clad in livelier hues; and ocean sings her ancient song to a more profound and haunting rhythm when the greatness and mystery of Nature have been interpreted to us by a mind kindred to her power and her charms.

This is a great conception of literature ; it is setting the claims and functions of literature very high. But they ought to be set high, however much the actuality may shrink by contrast.

It must be confessed that when we look round us in Ireland and compare the ideal with the real the effect is disheartening, or at the best we may say that, if it gives room for hope, it gives very little for satisfaction. We produce but little that is great, and the little that we do produce is recognised and applauded anywhere rather than here. When I take up a work, say of Rudyard Kipling's, and note the power and the clean vigorous finish of the style, the strong unfailing grasp of the subject, the creative imagination, and, in poetry, the magnificent poise and sweep of the rhythm, daring, yet graceful as a seabird's flight ; or when I read William Watson, and enjoy the stately serenity of his verse, and the gracious and noble conceptions that grow, touch by touch, before the reader's eye as, with sure and quiet hand, he clothes them with shape and form ; or when, to keep still to the younger men of the rising generation, I take up some poem of John Davidson's, with its penetrating thought, its dazzling imaginations, and its rich and haunting melody, and when, in addition to all these manifestations of grace and power, I note that the conception of fatherland, the love and pride in England, form an animating impulse that throbs like a beating heart through all their work and tinges it with the hues of heroic passion, then indeed I feel the poverty of our country far more acutely than when I compare our decayed cities and empty harbours with England's palaces and her swarming workshops and her estuaries thronged with the commerce of the world.

I would not be taken as asserting that we have nothing of worth to set over against the literary wealth of England. Of native power we have a considerable share, and if there is no steady glow of poetic fire there are at any rate flashes of great brilliance. I shall come later on to a discussion of some of the prominent figures in our literary movement of to-day ; but first I would wish to touch very briefly on the origin and conditioning circumstances of what is called the Irish Literary Revival of the present day.

' Revival ', to begin with, is, I think, a misnomer. It means the bringing to life again of something dead, or apparently dead, but which once had life and vigour. But Irish literature, in the sense in which we now use the term, never lived till now. I must explain a little of what I mean by this. In very early days Ireland had a literature in which there were many features of heroic greatness—a literature so old that the language in which its earliest works were written had become antiquated and obscure at the time when the first dawnings of French, or German, or English literature began to make their appearance. Amid strife and tumult, confusion and change, this literature, written in the vernacular Gaelic, lived on ; and in songs, romances, and chronicles it came down nearly to our own day. But in the meantime another race with another civilisation and another language entered Ireland, made themselves at home there, and in the course of time they too began to produce a literature, written in the English tongue, and having no connection whatever with the stream of Gaelic literature which followed on for a time beside it.

Now, neither of these literatures was at all adequate as an expression of the best thoughts and feelings of the nation. Education was forbidden to the Gaelic-speaking Irishman, and the development of the language was arrested. It remained in a childlike condition, fit enough for the needs of a simple pastoral people, but out of touch with European culture and incapable of being used as an instrument of modern thought and criticism. Anglo-Irish literature, on the other hand, powerful as it was in the hands of Swift, profound in those of Berkeley, brilliant in those of Lever, was as incapable as the Gaelic of filling the place of a national literature for Ireland. And this was because, if it flowered in Ireland, it struck its roots in another land. As Irish literature it had no past, no traditions ; utterly ignorant of the Gaelic, it was isolated from all that was deep, permanent, and characteristic in Irish thought and feeling, and, while often intensely patriotic—in the sense at least that it was anti-English —there was nothing in it to increase the national sense of dignity and self-reliance. They might defend and champion the Celt—those brilliant Anglo-Irish writers—and they often did so ; but it was as Wilberforce championing the West Indian slave ; they had little in common with him ; they could not share his memories ; they could not share his aspirations ; the iron of their bondage had never entered into his soul, nor could he discern the invisible bonds that held them after the material bonds had been struck off.

These two streams of literature, the Gaelic and the Anglo-Irish, flowed beside each other without intermixing until at last the hour of doom struck for the Gaelic language. This is one of the most curious phenomena in the history of the country, and a full account of it has never been written, and perhaps cannot be. The facts are, simply, that the language that had been spoken over the length and breadth of the land for at least fifteen centuries disappeared in about two generations as though it had no more vitality than a rootless flower in a child's garden. It is not my business here to go into the causes and significance of this very strange and very significant fact ; I will only point out that it *is* a fact and that, although Gaelic may still linger on our western seaboard, among a people who are unable to write the language they speak, it is for all practical purposes gone, and gone for ever.[1] Whether it would be desirable to revive it or not, it remains pretty certain that the people who allowed it to perish when they could easily have preserved it need not be expected to make the self-sacrificing and strenuous efforts which would now be necessary to re-establish it.

For good or ill, then, English has to be henceforward the medium of the expression of our ideas, our feelings, our character, our whole outlook upon the world of Nature and the world of man. When this became clear the question began to press itself upon many minds : ' If English is henceforward the language of Irish literature, can nothing be done to weave

---

[1] There were at that time about 20,000 people in the West of Ireland who could speak no English.

into it something of the spirit and flavour of the dying Gaelic tongue, and something also of the substance of the vast Gaelic literature so soon to take its place upon the dusty shelves of our libraries, when no one but an occasional student of philology will ever dream of disturbing its repose?' This was a question of profound importance, for it simply meant : ' Was Anglo-Irish literature henceforward to be, as it had been in the past, simply a reflection of the great body of English literature across the Channel, and the expression of a small dominant caste, or was it to be something native to Ireland, rooted in Ireland, drawing nourishment from the sources of an immemorial past, and, as it were, re-dedicating to the uses of a New Ireland the old myths, the old fancies, the old aspirations and conceptions, the natural features of the country so closely twined with the records of the past, and the great scenes and characters from ancient and legendary history on which the hand of the dying Gaelic literature had long ago laid its consecrating touch ! ' This is the meaning of the Irish Literary Revival of the present day, and this is the source of both its weakness and its strength. It is not part of the main current of English literature ; it is not trying to express the ideas and emotions current in England, handed down by the traditions of English literature and closely interwoven with the very texture of the English language. On the contrary it is endeavouring to take up the thread of another literature written in a far other tongue, obeying far other laws, full of conceptions strange to English literature, and of characters whose very names are difficult to represent in the English tongue.

Is it any wonder then that our modern Anglo-Irish literature stumbles, stammers, and hesitates, makes experiments that sometimes succeed and sometimes fail, that, in that respect, it bears all the marks of immaturity and crudity? But its performance up to the present is poor just because the task it has undertaken is so great. It has never produced a Swift, a Goldsmith, a Berkeley, or a Lever ; but, if it accomplishes its mission, it *will* produce writers who will be far closer and dearer to the Irish people than all these brilliant and powerful writers ever were or ever could be, for they will be Irish of the Irish. In their thinking they will attack the problems of life from our historic standpoint, and in their poetry their music will be tuned to the key to which the chords of the Gaelic heart will respond.

And now I shall leave these abstract questions and come to concrete examples by which I may illustrate what I am trying to express. I have said that the modern Irish literary movement represented an attempt to maintain the continuity of our literature by attaching itself to the existing Gaelic literature and absorbing whatever it could of the spirit and substance of that. Whether this intention was actually present and defined in the minds of the originators of our modern movement it is hard to say, but the movement becomes all the more important and real if the need of it should appear to have been felt only instinctively. That in some fashion or other it was felt it is hardly possible to doubt, in view of the fact that it was about the time of the middle of this century, when the Gaelic language was in the midst of its rapid dissolution, that the new movement first made its appearance.

Three men must be named, though there are many others who might be, in connection with the origin of the movement—Thomas Davis, James Clarence Mangan, and Samuel Ferguson. Davis's own work was more in the direction of pointing out the way for others and inspiring them to follow it, than of actually treading it himself. Though his poems are studded with phrases of Gaelic it was but rarely that he caught anything of the genuine Celtic flavour in his verse. The ' Lament for Owen Roe ' is, indeed, the only poem I can call to mind which could not have been written by anyone but a Celt. His prose criticisms were, however, of incalculable value to the movement and he must always be named among its originators. The work of Mangan and Ferguson, however, was entirely creative. In Mangan's most characteristic poems, such as the ' Lament for The Maguire ', ' Dark Rosaleen ', ' Siberia ', and ' The Women of Three Cows ', the Gaelic flavour is evident, and the dullest reader could hardly fail to see that with work of this kind a new spirit, a wild and foreign strain, had come into the English language ; and not only the new flavour but new scenes and characters. For instance, suppose an English poet— or an Irish one nurtured entirely on English literary traditions—wishes to take some great historical example of departed greatness and vigour ; he will think, like William Watson, of Henry V, or, like Swinburne, of Elizabeth. But what says Mangan ?

He sleeps, the great O'Sullivan, where thunder cannot rouse.

And this comes home to us ; this reaches the Irish heart. That one line ! What a vista of history it calls up ; and with what associations of dignity it invests the career of the indomitable chief of Dunboy ! In certain respects I think the work of Mangan has never been equalled by any later writer ; its beautiful and intricate melodic structure and its intensity of feeling are unsurpassed, and perhaps unsurpassable. But unfortunately the work which exhibits these fine qualities is comparatively small in quantity. He wrote often when he was not in the mood to write, and his verse was then bald and vapid, mere empty words. Even at his best, moreover, his range of feeling, intense though it was, was narrow. His conceptions were strange, unearthly, and morbid, partly the fruit of his wretched life and weak character.

Ferguson, however, a name never to be mentioned among Irishmen without veneration, if he lacked some of the things that Mangan had— such as delicate and exquisite music and diction, and lyrical intensity of passion—had nearly everything that Mangan lacked ; and I think it is on Ferguson that we must look as the true father and originator of the movement we are carrying on to-day. He had the great advantage, which Mangan had not, of a deep knowledge of the Celtic language and literature, and he had, too, what Mangan also lacked—the general culture, and especially the training in the classical languages, which will never make a man a poet, which a man may be a poet without possessing, but which always adds strength to the strong. Ferguson was the first writer who saw the greatness of our early Gaelic literature, and who was able to transmute it on any large scale into the new medium of expression. With him a whole crowd of new figures entered into Anglo-Irish literature : Cuchullin, Maeve, Fergus MacRoy, Mesgedra, Deirdre, and so forth ; and when they came they did not come, as some of them occasionally did in the poetry of Moore, in the garb and with the air of eighteenth-century courtiers and princesses, but with all their barbaric splendour about them, their native Celtic ways and thoughts, their fierce passions, their cruelty, their wild generosity and chivalry. And the manner of Ferguson's poems is as native, as original as the substance. The cadence of its music, the turns of expression, the epithets, the metaphors, all carry with them the Gaelic flavour.

Having said so much in praise of Ferguson, let us turn to the other side and see what we have to set against his great achievements. Those achievements were as great, I think, in their own way, as anything could well be, but there are not enough of them. This was really not Ferguson's fault so much as that of his country and his time. There was practically no audience for him. The opinion of the educated classes in Ireland, then as now, was extremely indifferent, to say the least of it, to anything that did not bear the hall-mark of English culture. Thomas Davis, Charles Duffy, John Mitchell, and other writers of the *Nation*, and I may add also the editors of the *Dublin University Review*, were, it is true, working hard and with growing success to inspire the Irish educated classes with at least a sufficient amount of Irish feeling to appreciate Irish literature ; but their work was swept away by the famine years, which were the tomb of so much that was promising and hopeful in Ireland ; and, though Ferguson went on producing poetry and at rare intervals published small volumes —his last work being brought out so lately as 1886—he never received one-tenth part of the recognition, the applause, and the serious and well-considered criticism that were his right.

In the class with which he was mainly associated he was looked on as a very worthy gentleman who filled certain public offices with credit and dignity, who had done sound and original work in deciphering Ogham inscriptions, and who occasionally amused his leisure hours by composing verses which very few people ever read, and which still fewer people, if any at all, would dream of considering in the light of an important contribution to literature. This was, and this is, the prevalent opinion about Ferguson in the classes I refer to, and as for the great mass of Celtic Ireland outside the cultivated classes, they never heard of him at all. This state of things is fortunately undergoing a change at present, and the fact that Messrs. Sealy, Bryers, and Walker have found it possible to bring out a cheap edition of Ferguson's ' Lays of the Western Gael ' is a significant and hopeful sign. But the fact remains that during Ferguson's lifetime he lived and wrote to all appearance in vain. To write at all so much and so well as he did, under such conditions, betokens a profound faith in the future of Irish literature, a faith which it remains for our own and other generations to justify.

I come next to a writer nearer our own day—in fact, entirely of our own day—but whose work was well begun before Ferguson's had ended. I refer to Standish O'Grady. His *History of Ireland*—a perverse and unfortunate title, for it has scarcely anything to do with history—appeared in the year 1875, and since then we have had from his pen another book in which he has achieved a real, a great, success, and a number of other books in which he has more or less dimly suggested what he could do if he tried. Leaving aside Ferguson, who, as the father and fountain-head of all our work, may be placed outside all comparison, I do not think there is any other writer to whom the modern Irish literary movement is so deeply indebted as it is to Standish O'Grady. The imaginative power with which, in his first book—the so-called ' History '—O'Grady tells the marvellous story of the life and death of Cuchullin, the Irish Achilles, would make a dozen successful and interesting books, as books go now. That whole region of things was, in spite of Ferguson, becoming the prey of the antiquarian. O'Grady lifted it again into the sphere of poetry. The shadowy gods and warriors ceased to be mere names ; they took heroic shape and form. They were filled with passions, terrific and super-human sometimes, but profoundly moving. Anger was there, and vengeance, malice and craft, honour and loyalty, self-sacrifice and devotion, and at times a pathos and tenderness which, in their poignant keenness, matched the gigantic scale on which all the passions of this early legendary age were conceived.

This was the first book I ever read which convinced me that there was such a thing as a spiritual Ireland, not only a material piece of the earth's surface called by that name, and I believe I may safely say that this has been its effect on very many other readers. But, looking at it from another point of view, and discounting the exaggerated emotion that must attach more or less to what is practically a new discovery, I must say that it was on the whole a book of promise rather than of final and perfect achievement. One read it with delight, with enchantment, and then one said, ' What a book O'Grady could write, if he liked, on the story of the Irish Iliad, the Wars of the Red Branch, and Queen Maeve ! ' The chief defect in the book is its utterly chaotic arrangement. Beside the magnificent story of Cuchullin, with which the book is mainly concerned, the attention is distracted by bits of irrelevant history and ethnology, and even geology, and of legends which have nothing to do with the main business of the work. The science is, I believe, altogether wrong as science ; but that is not the point. It has no business there at all. We do not want to consider whether Cuchullin was a Basque or a Finn, nor does it delight us to find him embedded like a fossil in the Pleistocene strata, into which we are plunged at the beginning of O'Grady's book. Taken all round the book reads too much like a collection of sketches and studies written at different times and with different ideas or purposes ; it is as if a man dug his hand into a pit of gold and jewels and brought out a handful to show us, instead of choosing with care and pains and many rejections and hesitations what would suit his purpose best, and ranging them, with long and patient workmanship, into the form of noble and beautiful ornaments such as are sometimes found in our bogs and on our seashores—relics of a day when Irish craftsmen worked for eternity.

But one work which may, I think, be called perfect and finished O'Grady has produced, and it will always be a source of pleasure to me personally to think that I had something to do with giving it to the world. My own contributions to the Irish literary movement have not been, or have only been very slightly, of a literary character, though in other ways I devoted to it for some years the best powers I had. Among the things I helped to give was O'Grady's *The Bog of Stars*, published in the New Irish Library. I do not know that anyone else has given it anything better than that. It is a collection of historical tales relating to Elizabethan Ireland, and it puts before us in so masterly and illuminating a way the characters and scenes and forces of the time that it suggests only one comparison; it suggests that O'Grady could be to Ireland what Walter Scott was to his country, or perhaps I might add what Rudyard Kipling in our own day is to the Indian Empire. The best of these tales of O'Grady's, ' The Bog of Stars ', which gives its title to the book, or ' Kiegangair ', or the tale of ' Rory Oge O'More ', seem to me as finished as anything that Kipling, the greatest living writer of short stories in English, has ever done.

But, alas! How much remains to be said before we can make that comparison complete! Kipling gave us a book as big as *The Bog of Stars* in 1891. It was received first with hesitation, then with recognition and delight. And then there came another, just as big and just as good, or better. And then another, and another, and another, each of them improving every time until at last we got to know the aspect of the Indian Empire, with its officials and natives, its gorgeous cities, its scenery, ways, and customs and character as well as we know our own. And consider the wonderful labour there is in these brilliant stories! There is no facile or hurried production here. These stories, as we know, are written and re-written five, six, seven times before they ever come into print. They are filed and polished, cut down here and expanded there, arranged and re-arranged, every word and every phrase considered, and every part toiled over until the tide of imagination is forced to run through every ramification of every vein in the work, and there is not a sentence, not a word in it, that is not quick with pulsating life. That is the way in which a great and worthy national literature is written, not by an occasional spurt or a flash of desultory genius.

Turn now to O'Grady's work. What has he given us since *The Bog of Stars* which contained so striking a revelation of power? We have had simply a couple of boys' stories, very readable and enjoyable no doubt, but hardly to be regarded as contributions to Irish literature; and a sort of Irish history called *Ireland : Her Story*, which, brilliant and suggestive as it is in parts, reads as if it had been written in six weeks. And this in spite of the fact that there is work lying ready to O'Grady's hand which no one but himself can do. He owes us a complete prose epic of Cuchullin and a complete rendering of the saga of Red Hugh O'Donnell, for both of which little remains to be done beyond the putting carefully in order —not that I count that a small or easy thing—of materials already in print. These are books which, done as O'Grady could do them, would go far to put the strength and vitality of the modern Irish literary movement beyond all question. But they still remain in the ' land of promise ' and, meantime, the years are slipping by which must decide whether there is to be a real ' Ireland ' here at all or only an English province.

It is impossible in the time at my disposal even to name anything like all the writers of merit who are playing their parts in the Irish intellectual movement of to-day ; therefore I have thought it best to deal rather fully with only a few principal and typical names. I must, however, at least mention Miss Katherine Tynan, now Mrs. Hinkson, who, both in prose and verse, has done much fine and characteristic work ; Miss Jane Barlow, whose idylls of Irish peasant life are like Carleton's without his grimness. Standish Hayes O'Grady, Dr. P. W. Joyce, and Dr. Douglas Hyde, all of whom have done work in the direct communication of Gaelic originals for which we cannot be too grateful ; Dr. Todhunter, who, in a little-known work named *The Banshee*, has treated two well-known Irish legends in a manner of singular and characteristic beauty ; Dr. George Sigerson, author of poems and criticism of which we can only regret we have not more ; Aubrey de Vere, whose ' Bard Ethell ' and some shorter pieces like the ' Wedding of the Clans ', are true to the Gaelic ear ; A. P. Graves, who has accomplished so much for Irish song and music ; and Miss Margaret Stokes, who has done memorable and enduring work on the subject of early Irish art and the history connected with it.

There is, however, another writer who has devoted himself to creative work with so firm a purpose, so high a spirit, and so much success that he cannot be passed over in a sentence and indeed he deserves much fuller treatment than I am now able to give him. This is William Butler Yeats. Yeats, I think, is the best example we have of an Irish poet who takes his work as seriously as the best English writers do and who lets nothing leave his hand that he knows how to improve. And he has his reward. Whether he is read and admired in Ireland it is impossible to say, owing to our lack of organs of literary criticism. But across the Channel journals like the *Daily Chronicle* and the *Athenaeum*, recognised leaders of opinion, place Yeats in the very first rank of living poets who write in the English tongue. And I think it is worth noticing that the intensely Irish quality attaching both to his style and his themes have not in the least prevented this cordial and ungrudging recognition of his power by the great English journals.

Yeats has done excellent and memorable work both in prose and in poetry, but poetry is his main business. It is by this that his place in literature will be fixed. What that place may be it is very hard to say. He is a young man still. His career may, I think, practically be said to lie before him and he has given evidence of such varied powers and such a reserve of power that I should think it very hard to judge from what he has already done of the character that his future work may assume. A reader who had read only a dozen or so of his poems from the *Wanderings of Oisin* or the *Countess Cathleen* might put him down as a mystic, interested in nothing but the working of spiritual forces which he expressed in beautiful and imaginative but very obscure language. Such a reader would be quite unprepared for the fine and close observation and idealisation of the common things of life shown in Yeats' little prose novelette *John Sherman,* or for the vein of delicate and quiet but genuine humour apparent in some of the tales in his *Celtic Twilight.*

I may say this much, however : that Yeats's turn for mysticism, though it has produced much beautiful and interesting work, is a very real danger to him. Not that I object to mysticism in itself, for we Irish are all mystics in a sense, and a very real sense. You must either be a mystic or an atheist.

But by mysticism in literature I mean the description of the working of spiritual forces in the technical language of a recondite system of philosophy and not in language that goes home to the bosoms and brains of ordinary men and women. I won't go so far as to say that great poetry is always written in simple language, but I will certainly maintain that great poetry is not written in technical language. Here is an instance of what I mean ; this is a short poem contributed by Yeats to the January number of the *New Review* and entitled ' Everlasting Voices ' :

> O sweet, everlasting voices, be still :
> Go to the guards of the heavenly fold,
> And bid them wander, obeying your will,
> Flame under flame till time be no more.
> Have you not heard that our hearts are old,
> That you call in birds, in wind on the hill,
> In shaken boughs, in tide on the shore ?
> O sweet, everlasting voices, be still !

This poem is exquisite in phrase and melody, and one reads it the first time for the sheer enjoyment of the music, but then one asks oneself what it means. Now, thanks to some acquaintance with the very obscure philosophic systems of which Yeats is a passionate student—an acquaintance due to the personal friendship with Yeats to which I am proud to be able to lay claim—I did, on a sixth reading, or thereabouts, begin to have some very faint and shadowy conception of what Yeats was, to use a vulgar phrase, ' driving at ' in those lines ; but I could not explain them without writing an essay to do so, and I cannot believe that people unprepared by special studies would be capable—to use another vulgar phrase—of making head or tail of them. This is a defect in Yeats, for, other things being equal, it *is* a defect and not a merit in a poem that nobody can understand it.

To show how perfectly Yeats can succeed in quite a different and, I think, a more difficult vein, let me quote these two lovely stanzas, called ' An Old Song Re-sung ' :

> Down in the sally gardens my love and I did meet,
> She passed the sally gardens with little snow-white feet.
> She bade me take love easy as leaves grow on the tree,
> But I, being young and foolish, with her would not agree.
>
> In a field by the river my love and I did stand,
> And on my leaning shoulder she laid her snow-white hand.
> She bade me take life easy as grass grows on the weirs,
> But I was young and foolish and now am full of tears.

That is a little jewel of poetry, of ' purest ray serene ', and I hope and believe that Yeats has many more such in his treasury.

Before I close I want to ask your attention for a side of my subject which I have hardly touched on yet. A literary movement is not made up only of literateurs. It would be a very poor and barren affair if it was. You must have readers as well as writers, critics as well as creators, and behind the writers you must have a national force that buoys them up and gives them the assurance that they are writing for generations yet unborn.

How do we stand as regards the audience for Irish literature ? I fear but badly. I cannot disguise the fact that the outlook here is gloomy. Our literary societies are a symptom of a certain stir of life among the young men of the present day, but they hardly affect the nation outside a couple of towns ; and as long as we have little or nothing that can be called an organ of well-considered and scholarly criticism—and that an organ with influence and plenty of readers—the Irish literary movement will work at a great disadvantage and will tend to centre more and more, as it is now visibly doing, on London and to get out of touch with Ireland. We need altogether in some way or other a greater cultivation of the critical spirit to enable us to distinguish between the patient and lasting work of the true genius and the flashy and facile imitation of it in which we Irish are unfortunately so successful. And until we get it, genius in Ireland will work under very discouraging conditions.

Furthermore we need, as I have said, more national spirit among the people. I do not speak here in any political sense. I mean a spirit such as can be shared, and often is shared, by Unionists and Home Rulers alike. Here I think the outlook is gloomier still. It is impossible to forget—one cannot forget—the manner in which the Irish people gave up practically without a struggle what they should have considered as their most precious possession—the proud and sure seal of their nationality—the language their forefathers had spoken on this soil for fifteen hundred years. Nor can one overlook the fact that, while we have in the present day a movement, more or less fluctuating in its vigour, in favour of transferring the seat of Irish legislature from London to Dublin, we have also a movement which, through a thousand invisible agencies, is working out with unremitting energy and success the thorough anglicisation of the spirit of this country, and which is imposing on us not only the language, but also the manners, the social and political ideas, and in fact the whole civilisation of the English ; of which civilisation we are absorbing the worst features with the greatest readiness.

To give an example of what I mean. A friend of mine was present not long ago at a merry-making among some Kerry peasantry, who were assembled around a bonfire, and had songs and other amusements. Of all the songs performed there only one was an Irish song, and that was contributed by my friend himself—the descendant, I may add, of a Cromwellian settler ! The rest were ' Two lovely black eyes ', ' The Man that broke the Bank at Monte Carlo ', ' Says the Old Obadiah ', and all the current vulgarities of the English music-halls.

There, among a hundred other signs and symptoms, you observe the counter-movement that is going on alongside our Irish literary movement ; and I think it is by no means certain which will win. We, who are working for the literary movement, may be the advance guard of a victorious army, the pioneers of a new and glorious epoch ; or we may, perchance, be only firing the last few shots of a defeated force. Our poetry may be a vision of heavenly promise, or it may be but a thin phantom lingering for a while over the grave of Gaelic Ireland.

It must be left for other generations to say with certainty what we are and what we are doing. It is for us to compel them, if they notice us at all, to say at least that we did manfully and with pure, liberal, and upright aims the work which our time and our land appeared to lay upon us.

My father was severely taken to task in some quarters for his remarks in this address about the Irish language and some rather heated newspaper correspondence resulted. Rolleston's contention was that, as the language had been allowed to fall into disuse, it had not kept up with modern scientific and other developments and that therefore, if it were to be brought up to date and made to serve modern needs, it would be obliged to coin a mass of new words which could only be purely arbitrary creations and which would, when grafted on to the existing language, deprive the latter of that individuality and character which a language can only acquire satisfactorily by a process of natural and continuous evolution. Others, on the contrary, maintained that the Irish language could cope with any demand that might be made upon it and I even heard fanatics on the subject state quite seriously that it was destined to be the one universal language, achieving the objects its inventors designed Esperanto to fulfil.

The upshot of these criticisms is related by Dr. Douglas Hyde in his book, *Myself and the League*, which was published in Irish early in 1938. I am greatly indebted to my friend, Donal O'Sullivan, for this translation, and to Dr. Hyde for permission to use it.

The Gaelic League was only two or three years old when my good friend, T. W. Rolleston, raised a great controversy by a speech which he delivered to the Press Club. In that speech he said a good many things with which the Gaelic League did not agree, and he drew upon himself abusive letters in the press. But the principal thing he said was that it was impossible to employ Irish as a medium of expression for contemporary ideas and contemporary criticism. There was a meeting of the League Council on 1st February, 1896, and John MacNeill answered Rolleston on every point. A letter was read from Rolleston himself and he defended himself on the arguments adduced against him ; at the same time he said that he was ready and willing to choose a short literary passage out of some scientific work in English, that he should give it to me to translate into Irish, and for me to return it to him, when he would give my Irish version to another Irish scholar for him to render into English again. ' We shall then print the two versions—the original English and the translation from the Irish—in the Claidheamh Soluis (the weekly organ of the Gaelic League) and the public will see whether the language is suited or not to present-day affairs. If this experiment proves more favourable to Irish than I imagine it will, I shall change my mind and freely admit that I was mistaken.'

I agreed to this proposal, and a short time later I received two pieces of English from him, one of them taken, if my memory serves me, from a scientific work on crustacea, and the other, I think, was selected from Herbert Spencer. It did not take me long to translate them into Irish, and I returned them to Rolleston. He then gave my Irish to John MacNeill for him to translate into English. The latter did so, and gave the papers back to Rolleston. Rolleston was astonished to find that the translation which MacNeill had made was just as good as the original English, or in places better, for it was clearer. We had failed in one word only. At all events Rolleston was completely satisfied by the result of the experiment, and hastened to proclaim the fact.

It should not be inferred, however, from this incident that my father was in any sense an enemy of the Irish language. Far from it ; but he did not subscribe to the ridiculous claims that were made for it in some quarters, nor did he wish people to learn it for other than sentimental reasons and because it opened up the way to a first-hand knowledge and understand-ing of the past greatness of Irish literature.

The address in other respects made a profound impression not only on those who actually heard it but on others who read it afterwards. It was delivered only three years after the foundation of the Irish Literary Society which had in 1893 placed on record its members' appreciation of what Rolleston had done for the new literary movement by present-ing him with a valuable gift and an illuminated address. In this he was referred to as the ' virtual founder ' of the Society and it is evident that he had by 1896 become the actual leader of the movement. Is it any wonder that the Irish writers, having had such a plan of campaign mapped out for them by a General of such outstanding qualifications, should have turned on every possible occasion to ' T. W. R.' when they felt the need for advice or guidance ? Come to him they certainly did and found the warmest welcome and every help they could have desired.

This address defines in fact what was actually Rolleston's niche in the Irish literary movement. He was the practical man, the organizer of victory, the man who thought things out, who directed the human forces which had fallen naturally under his influence, who told each to what particular end his own particular talents might best be directed, and who spurred on the whole army—for such it became—to that achievement which gave to the Ireland they all loved a modern literature based on the immortal tales of past glories and the hopes for a still more glorious future.

How could a movement impelled by such inspiration from its head and with such practical advice and scathing criticism ready to its hand fail to prosper ? Prosper it did, with the result that the English language acquired, in the hands of the Irish writers, a new dignity, a new rhythm, and a fresh beauty that are really a legacy from the old Irish language. Some of the greatest writers in the English language are, or were, Irishmen—W. B. Yeats, George Russell, George Moore, James Stephens, Denis Johnston, Sean O'Casey, Liam O'Flaherty—and the foundations on which they built their individual achievements were laid in Dublin by the Irish Literary Society in general and by T. W. Rolleston in particular.

George Moore, though one of the most frequent visitors to our house in Pembroke Road in those days, was actually only on the fringe of the movement and George Bernard Shaw did not belong to the movement at all ; essentially an individualist he struck out a line of his own in which his success has been phenomenal and well-deserved, but which owes nothing to the influence of Ireland's Literary Renaissance.

St. John Ervine too, the brilliant Irish playwright and dramatic critic, cannot be said to be a product of the movement, though he was for a short time Director of the Abbey Theatre.

O'Grady did write the Cuchullin Saga—in three volumes—and made a masterly job of it. Yeats, though always remaining somewhat of a mystic, took the advice given by Rolleston and spent the last forty years of his life passing meteor-like from magnitude to magnitude in the Anglo-Irish literary firmament.

My father's admiration for the work of W. B. Yeats was no new thing at the time he put his plan of campaign before the Irish writers. In 1885 and 1886 he had been Editor of the *Dublin University Review*, and in that publication he had included the first of Yeats's works ever to appear in print. This was *The Island of Statues*. His friendship with Yeats was of very long standing and the great poet stands out most prominently of all perhaps in my own recollection of those warriors of the Irish Literary Revival. Next in order of vividness would come Standish O'Grady, George Russell ('AE'), and George Moore. Yeats was tall and had an athletic figure in spite of a marked stoop. His hair was jet black and generally long ; he wore it brushed low across his forehead, a habit which gave him a slightly sinister appearance, which seemed to be accentuated by his pince-nez, with their broad black ribbon, and very piercing eyes. I think we children were a little afraid of him and I know we were distinctly timorous where 'AE' was concerned. We called him 'The Tappy Man' because we believed him to be capable of peopling a house with ghosts and fairies whenever he wished and to be able to produce mysterious rappings and tappings behind the wall of a room.

But we children were not the only persons on whom George Russell made the same kind of impression. I have mentioned that my father's second wife was Maud Brooke, daughter of another great Irishman, the Reverend Stopford Brooke. She has very kindly allowed me to read some of her famous father's private diaries, in particular that for the year 1898 when he came to preach in Dublin and to visit his brothers and sisters and ourselves. This is an entry in his diary for Monday, 6 June, in that year :

George Russell, the Irish poet, came in to dine. And he talked—opalescently. George Russell has more stuff in him than Lionel Johnson, but he talked very sad stuff about his spiritualistic experiences, his visions, dreams, and phantasms. Everything he saw was either opalescent or iridescent, and I wished at times he would opalescence himself into an iridescent vision. At last I could stand it no longer, and I went to bed, and read his poetry. It, like Johnson's, wavered from phantom to phantom of feeling, without a shred of fine matter, all a-tremble with unfelt emotion, all made up of a few properties shaken together into rhyme and pretty-coloured words. 'Tis like a kaleidoscope ; all sorts of patterns turn up, but there are only a few pieces of glass.

Then again a fortnight later :

G. Russell came in. Rain all day. G. Russell's chief word is 'opalescent', and we waited, intent, till it should appear. Appear it did within five minutes, and then in every second sentence. I wished I had an opal for every time he used it. It is apparently the colour of all visitants from the spiritual world, and in order to show off, they always take care, according to Russell, to have a background of purple and violet cloud, before which they sway, like Nautch girls, and then rise and waver into iridescent vapour which floats into infinite space. I understood, but vaguely, that Russell opalesced his soul through the top of his head and accomplished

104, PEMBROKE ROAD, DUBLIN

UNION AND IRISH FLAGS IN HONOUR OF QUEEN VICTORIA'S
VISIT IN 1900

G W. RUSSELL ('AE'), 1901

one of these spiritual spirals into space. What he did there, what the spiral did, I couldn't comprehend, but it seemed to be naughty. It must be funny to rise in immeasurable space.

Yet this man is an admirable organiser of the Irish Industries, knows his Ireland well, has just views of how to lift the Irish peasant out of pauperism and carries them out with skill and wisdom.

If ' AE ' impressed Stopford Brooke in that way is it any wonder that we were a bit scared of him ? I was ten at the time the above diary entries were made and my sister, Una, was little more than a year older.

Another entry in Stopford Brooke's diary gives a vivid impression of the Irish writers *en masse* ; this refers to an evening party at 104 Pembroke Road :

Maud had a party of about 100 people in the evening. O'Leary, L. La Touche, Emily La Naize, and a host of folk were there whom I had known young . . . O'Leary belongs to another world, like an Enoch Arden who has been half a century alone—like a Spanish galleon in a modern fleet. His chief pleasure is in buying ancient books, dusty, dog-eared, worn to shreds, and he lives among them in decay. Yet his soul is young and his eyes pathetic, and his long white beard flows down his chest like a white cataract. Mr. Power, the great whiskey man, talked to me. ' What ! ' he said, ' Are you a clergyman ? ' And he asked me to lunch. Poets were scattered about the room like birches, thin, waving things, hungry for subjects ; diaphanous bodies, iridescent eyes, each believing himself to be a re-incarnation of Shelley with an additional touch of genius. Journalists ran hither and thither questing, like dogs in a covert. Maud received well and looked royally.

For Standish O'Grady we felt no sort of awe at all ; where others, as the result perhaps of their own intense earnestness, seemed to have grown old before their time, O'Grady, the doyen of them all—except O'Leary—had remained essentially youthful. Had Peter Pan been created in those days he would undoubtedly have been called the Peter Pan of the Revival. There was nothing of the literary dreamer about O'Grady ; no more genial, friendly, open-hearted man ever lived and his appearance belied his great reputation as a scholar. He looked typically Irish ; in fact if one were to take the stage Irishman of the English music-halls of those days and remove all the coarseness that the English stage seemed to think it necessary to import in order to portray the character the result would have been Standish James O'Grady. While Russell, Yeats, Moore, yes, and my father too, seemed to live on a plane apart from ordinary people, Standish O'Grady belonged to our world and to our earth ; we worshipped the two books of adventure referred to in Rolleston's address, *Lost on Du-Corrig* and *The Chain of Gold*.   Yet in spite of his appearance and joviality, especially where children were concerned, it was O'Grady who pointed the way to the Irish Literary Revival, work for which he never received the financial reward it more than deserved.   He was awarded a Civil List Pension, the need for which should never have arisen.

Though eleven years older than Rolleston, O'Grady lived to write an appreciation of his life-long friend for the *Irish Times* when my father died in December, 1920 :

> I first met Rolleston one evening at Edward Dowden's. We took to each other at once and arranged for a long walking tour next day in the County Wicklow. It was the beginning of a friendship which has been one of the greatest pleasures of my life. I had heard of Rolleston before as very handsome, much devoted to poetry, and a good boxer ; and indeed all his life he was much inclined to manly physical exercises. I set him once to cleaving wood, which he did with a zest. Presently he leaned upon his axe and said to me, ' Honestly now, I'd rather earn my living by swinging an axe or some other kind of physical activity than by any kind of intellectual and sedentary labour. . . .'
>
> He was social, hospitable, always courteous and considerate to others, and very companionable. His spirits were not high but very equable ; he was ever cheerful and alert, always interested about something, and communicating his interest to others. Indeed such a combination of the man, the gentleman, the scholar, and the man of the world we are not likely to see again in Ireland, the times being more favourable to a type characterised by a fierce and uncompromising earnestness. . . .

How deplorably true is that last sentence !

The O'Gradys lived in Adelaide Road less than five minutes' walk from No. 5 Harcourt Terrace, the home of Mr. and Mrs. George Coffey and their son, Dermot. George Coffey and T. W. Rolleston were frequently mistaken for each other ; both were tall, striking-looking men, and both wore beards. Lady Fingall in her book of recollections, *Seventy Years Young*, writes regarding some tableaux at the Chief Secretary's Lodge based on Yeats's ' Countess Cathleen ', when this resemblance was useful :

> I was the Countess Cathleen, and I am sure I enjoyed it. . . . Constance [1] was the nurse ; and T. W. Rolleston and Dr. Coffey, the Keeper of Irish Antiquities at the Dublin Museum, were the two very handsome merchants who bargained for my soul.

---

[1] Lady Constance Lytton.

STANDISH O'GRADY, 1894

W. B. YEATS, 1894

My father, though he never attempted to write a play himself, was inevitably interested in the theatre as a means of expression and for telling a story. Shakespeare, of course, attracted him powerfully and the visits of Benson, Tree, and Forbes Robertson to Dublin were red-letter occasions. We were not allowed as children to go to a theatre to see anything except Shakespeare, though this rule had to be relaxed on one occasion when Miss Mollie Salmon, daughter of the exceedingly Reverend Dr. Salmon, Provost of Trinity College, came to tea at 104 Pembroke Road and announced that she was going to take us to the Pantomime ! Naturally this question had been raised before—by my sister and myself—but our proposal had been sternly vetoed. The invitation of the daughter of a Doctor of Divinity who was also Provost of Trinity was, however, a different matter, and the upshot of what at first looked to Una and myself as a bombshell was that not only were we allowed to go but father came too ! And enjoyed himself immensely. Perhaps I should add that Una and I had in no way prompted Miss Salmon ; we hadn't thought of it.

Equally vivid are my recollections of *Julius Caesar*, *The Tempest*, and *Hamlet*, and of Forbes Robertson and Gertrude Elliott in *The Light that Failed*, in favour of which the Shakespeare-only rule was also relaxed.

Among my father's friends in those days were Mr. and Mrs. George Pollock and their daughter, Rosie, who lived at Stillorgan just outside Dublin. They too were Shakespeare enthusiasts and held regular Shakespeare readings at their house, ' Oatlands '. It was on one of these evenings that my father met that gracious and human little lady, Miss Edith Badham —now Dr. Edith Badham, LL.D.—the Head Mistress and owner, with her sister, Alice, of an excellent school for girls in Mespil Road—St. Margaret's Hall. It was as a result of this meeting that my sister and I—small boys were taken in the lower forms—were sent to St. Margaret's Hall as our first school, a fact for which we shall always be grateful. We had the great pleasure recently of renewing acquaintance with Dr. Badham for, though ' Miss Alice ' has gone, St. Margaret's Hall and ' Miss Edith ' are still going strong.

George Coffey was an antiquarian and archaeologist rather than a writer, his literary output being almost entirely on the subject of Ireland's wealth of medieval, early Christian, and pre-historic monuments and works of art. He had, I think, an almost personal affection for the lovely things that were in his charge at the Museum, and the fact that he talked about them brilliantly when encouraged to do so made his closing days all the more sad ; he was stricken with paralysis which first deprived him of the power of speech.

The semi-theatrical occasion referred to by Lady Fingall brings back recollections of another venture in the theatre world with which T. W. R. was intimately connected ; in fact, as in so many Irish cultural matters, his were the driving power and energy that were mainly responsible for initiating a movement that was ultimately to carry Ireland and her legends and myths, and a knowledge of the Irish character, to the farthest corners of the world.

Besides writing stories and verse and history—mythological, legendary, and actual—the Irish writers were turning out plays, notably W. B. Yeats, Lady Gregory, and Edward Martyn. But no one was acting them, mainly perhaps because it was impossible to convince theatre owners that they would make money—that people would go to see them. As usual Rolleston came to the rescue, not with money, of which he had no more than any of his literary colleagues, but with organising ability, leadership, and encouragement. He formed a Dramatic Branch of the Irish Literary Society and, to cut a long story short, the Gaiety Theatre in Dublin was engaged for a week and for the first time in history Irish audiences saw Irish plays written by Irish authors and acted by Irishmen and Irish-women. It was a wonderful week, in which I think only one professional player took part [1] ; the remainder were all amateurs and included not only my father but that famous fire-brand, Maud Gonne, who made a remarkably handsome Queen Maeve.[2]

The children of the Irish writers, including myself, were roped in for the chorus, but we were not allowed to do any of the singing for reasons which, in my own case at any rate, were obvious ; we went through the motions while the actual vocal effects were produced by the Choir of St. Patrick's Cathedral stationed in the wings. I have often wondered if

---

[1] My recollection is that this was a Miss Sara Alcock.
[2] See page 40.

anyone saw through the deception. Money, of course, was not too plentiful, and for that reason it was not found possible to decorate both sides of our stage costumes with those beautiful designs and patterns with which the ancient Irish costumes were embellished. We had, therefore, to be careful to keep the decorated sides of our persons towards the audience. In one of the plays I was, by virtue of the fact that I was T. W. R'.s son, promoted to be Spear-bearer to the King, played by my father.

At that time I was a boy at school at Strangways, so the year must have been about 1899 or 1900, for in 1901 I followed in my father's footsteps and went to St. Columba's College at Rathfarnham, high up on the side of the Three Rock Mountain in the Dublin Hills. This school, a sister foundation of Radley, is still in the front rank of Public Schools and, though it is in Southern Ireland, does not seem to be suffering any disadvantage from that fact in spite of being strictly Protestant and intensely loyal to the British Empire.

That, however, is by the way. How that week of Irish plays turned out financially I do not know, but it set a match to a train that led eventually to the Abbey Theatre movement which was made possible by the energy of W. B. Yeats, who controlled it, and the generosity of Miss A. E. F. Horniman of Manchester, who supplied the finance. From the Abbey Theatre emerged the Irish Players whose renown is to-day world-wide. Without them and without the Abbey Theatre which gave them birth Synge might have had no cast for *The Playboy of the Western World*, nor Denis Johnston any inducement to write *The Moon on the Yellow River*, and Sean O'Casey's *Juno and the Paycock* would perhaps never have been written.

But Synge, O'Casey, and Johnston had not been heard of in the 'nineties and one may be permitted to wonder if they would ever have stepped before the curtain to answer the call of ' Author ' if it had not been for the literary and dramatic foundation-stones so well laid by Rolleston and his enthusiastic contemporaries. Probably they would have started to erect the edifice themselves ; they would have done it competently, but hardly better, for in the main the Irish playwrights as well as the Irish writers seem always to have kept in mind Stopford Brooke's dictum in the address with which he opened the inaugural meeting of the Irish Literary Society of London in 1893 :

> It is a patriot's work to manifest the beautiful things which his country has done, that he may be loved and honoured, and by that he glorifies his nation far more than by increasing her commerce.

The Chair at this inaugural meeting was taken by a cousin of the Rollestons who was doing and continued to do great work for Irish literature. He is best known wherever the English tongue is spoken and Irish songs are sung as the author of *Father O'Flynn*, but is perhaps less renowned as having for many years written the ' By the way ' column of the now defunct London *Globe*. This was one of the most famous columns of humour London has ever known ; there is nothing like it to-day.

The writer was the late Alfred Perceval Graves, M.A., whose collections of Irish songs and ballads constituted such splendid contributions to the literary movement. His first book, *Songs of Killarney*, appeared as long ago as 1873, and his last in 1916. The family's literary tradition is being carried on by his son, Robert, author of *Good-bye to all that* and *I, Claudius*, while a nephew, Sir Cecil Graves, K.C.M.G., is second-in-command of the British Broadcasting Corporation. T. W. Rolleston was Robert Graves's godfather.

Mention of the lighter side of literature as exemplified by the immortal *Father O'Flynn* leads naturally to another figure in the Dublin of the 'nineties and later. Though he can hardly be said to have contributed to the serious business of creating an Irish literature in the English tongue, he did do a vast amount to keep his contemporaries amused and to remind them on occasion that life has a more frivolous side ; this is something well worth doing and that lovable old character, Percy French, did it supremely well. He and Rolleston were the greatest of friends and scarcely a fortnight passed without a visit from him ; he lived barely fifteen minutes' walk away from us, in Mespil Road.

French was a writer of humorous songs in which, in the kindliest but most telling way, he took off many Irish characteristics and customs and foibles ; for these he composed simple tunes designed in the first place to be played as banjo accompaniments. I can see him now in our drawing-room in Pem-

DOUGLAS HYDE AND A. P. GRAVES, 1894

broke Road and again in Hampstead sitting forward in an arm-chair singing his own songs in a quiet Irish voice, now and then plucking the strings of his banjo, and conjuring up for us with a word and a gesture pictures of Irish characters and habits in a manner that only a completely humourless person could resist.

With the Irishman's usual disregard of the financial aspect of his work Percy French neglected to copyright his first song ; it was pirated in America and became almost immediately famous, but French got not a penny from it. The song was *Abdul, a Bul-bul Ameer* ; thank goodness the modern, generally nauseating, and frequently hopelessly ungrammatical ' popular ' song of to-day has not quite succeeded in killing old Abdul ; he is still heard of occasionally ' on the air ', though a more frequent visitor to that medium is the delightful Irish lad who visited London and wrote back good advice to his Mary, who lived ' where the Mountains of Mourne shweep down to the sea '. Percy French wrote the words of that song and his friend, Dr. Collinson, the music.

Another song, *The West Clare Railway*, nearly landed Percy French in the Courts as defendant in an action for libel. This was threatened by the Directors of the West Clare Railway, an actual going concern, but the rest of Ireland, which had laughed so heartily at the song, laughed again at the Directors. Their sense of humour eventually came to the rescue and I believe they ended by giving our old friend a grand dinner at Corless's.

> Are ye right there, Michael, are ye right ?
> Do ye think we'll get there before the night ?
> Oh, it's all depending whether the ould engine holds together,
> And it might now, Michael, so it might.

The assistance of the passengers was sometimes required for various jobs :

> At Lahinch the sea shines like a jewel,
> And with joy you are ready to shout ;
> But the stoker cries out ' There's no fuel,
> And the fire's taytotally out !
> But hand up that bit of a log there,
> I'll soon have ye out of the fix ;
> There's a fine clamp of turf in the bog there,
> And the rest go a-gathering sticks.'

4

The successful song-writer of to-day makes a fortune ;
Percy French made nothing ; he was always ' broke '.

And so the Irish Literary Revival grew and developed and
spread, and scattered its works and its stories and its poems
and plays over Ireland, then over England, and now over the
whole world.   The labour, largely of love, undertaken by the
original Revivalists was carried out to the accompaniment
of laughter and gaiety, yes, and of music too ; for in 1897
there was held in Dublin the first Feis Ceoil, a veritable Irish
Feast of Song, corresponding to the Welsh annual Eisteddfod.
This took place in the early summer of that year and its main
interest centred round Rolleston's *Deirdre Cantata*, the music
for which was composed by Signor M. Esposito.   The First
Prize at the Feis was awarded to this work.

Rolleston chose for his subject what is one of the most
heroic and it is certainly the saddest and most moving of
mythological stories—the tale of Deirdre and the Sons of Usna
—*Deirdre of the Sorrows*.   The story goes that Felim, son of Dall,
was entertaining King Conor of Ulster when news was brought
that his wife had borne him a daughter.   The Druid Cathbad
foretold that she should be the fairest of women but that,
through her, death and ruin would come upon Ulster.   Conor
thought he could avert this fate by keeping Deirdre, for that
was the name given to the child, carefully secluded from the
world till she was old enough for him to marry.   But, when
the time for the marriage was near, Deirdre, with the help
of her nurse, Levarcam, met Naisi, one of the three sons of
Usna, and fled with him and his brothers to Scotland, where
they lived for many years in Glen Etive, hunting and fishing
and seeing no one but each other and their servants.

Eventually Conor sent Fergus, son of Roy, to ask them to
come back to Ireland, when everything would be forgiven.
Deirdre was suspicious, but the others over-ruled her and they
all returned.   Deirdre, however, had been right ; the sons of
Usna were attacked by Conor with the aid of Owen, son of
Duracht, and killed.   The story ends thus in Rolleston's
re-telling of it in *The Myths and Legends of the Celtic Race* [1] :

Then Conor took Deirdre perforce, and for a year she abode with him
in the palace in Emain Macha, but during all that time she never smiled.

---

[1] George G. Harrap and Co., 1911.

At length Conor said : ' What is it that you hate most of all on earth, Deirdre ? ' And she said : ' Thou thyself and Owen, son of Duracht ', and Owen was standing by. ' Then thou shalt go to Owen for a year ', said Conor. But when Deirdre mounted the chariot behind Owen she kept her eyes on the ground, for she would not look on those who thus tormented her ; and Conor said, taunting her, ' Deirdre, the glance of thee between me and Owen is the glance of a ewe between two rams '. Then Deirdre started up, and, flinging herself headforemost from the chariot, she dashed her head against a rock and fell dead.

And when they buried her it is said there grew from her grave, and from Naisi's, two yew-trees, whose tops, when they were full grown, met each other over the roof of the great church of Armagh, and intertwined together, and none could part them.

Here is Rolleston's story in the Cantata of the fight in which Naisi and his brothers were slain :

> The last, last onset is now advancing,
>   A rain of lances, a storm of blows.
> Like pines in tempest the sons of Usna
>   Go down loud-crashing among their foes.
>
> Still, at last, is the roar of battle,
>   And Conor stands in the morning red,
> And gazes silent with old eyes weary
>   On Deirdre kneeling among her dead.

Then comes Deirdre's lament, every line vibrant with her great love for Naisi, her tremendous sorrow, and her hatred for the treacherous Conor :

> O sword of Naisi, ancient friend,
>   Deal yet one blow, the last and best ;
> And Deirdre to her lover send
>   To share his endless rest.
>
> The Lions from the hill are gone,
>   The Dragons from the cave are fled,
> The Eagles from the rock have flown,
>   The Mother wails her dead.
>
> O Sons of Usna, kind and brave,
>   Your glory shone from sea to sea.
> Would I were lying in my grave
>   Ere you had died for me.
>
> O Ye, who pay to each his due,
>   Have vengeance for this deed of bale
> Upon the traitor King who slew
>   The noblest of the Gael.

From age to age let glory grow
 Upon the fierce avenging hand
That heaps the measure of its woe
 Upon an impious land.

The Lions from the hill are fled,
 The Eagles from the rock have flown,
Soon, soon I join my sacred dead,
 And go where they have gone.

For Usna's sons make wide the tomb,
 O dig the grave both deep and wide,
Where Deirdre till the day of doom
 Shall sleep at Naisi's side.

Compared with many other poets T. W. Rolleston's output was not very great ; by far the best work he did was in the form of verse-narrative, all of which is singularly free from superfluities and goes smoothly on with the story it has to tell. It is as easy to read as prose without losing a fraction of the beauty and vividness that only great verse can impart to a really great story.

About Signor Esposito's music I cannot say anything with authority but it was very favourably received by the musical critics of the time. Perhaps the fact that Esposito was Sir Hamilton Harty's music teacher may be a sufficient recommendation.

It would not be possible here to traverse in any detail the subsequent history of the Irish Literary Revival. Rolleston, having seen the movement well under way and on the right course, and having watched the advent to it of J. M. Synge, Sean O'Casey, and others who might be called the second generation of the Revivalists, devoted himself more to other work.

Mention must be made, however, of one other celebrated Irish writer who is happily still living. This is the Reverend J. O. Hannay, who, as ' George A. Birmingham ', achieved fame as the author of *The Seething Pot, Hyacinth, Spanish Gold,* and other books, as well as that gorgeous comedy that only an Irishman could have conceived and that could only have had Ireland as its setting—*General John Regan.* I wrote to Hannay when I had made up my mind to try to put together these recollections of my father and to place on record his services to literature and to Ireland. Hannay's reply must speak for itself :

I am delighted to help in any way I can with the proposed life of your father, which, in my opinion, most certainly ought to be written.

The date of his going to Delgany I do not know.[1] I went there as curate in 1888 and found him resident in a small house where I often visited him.[2] A great friend of his at that time was Alfred de Burgh,[3] and they used to spend many evenings together reading Greek plays. I always yearned to be asked to join these parties, but never was, and, I think, quite rightly for I was not nearly as good a Greek scholar as either of them.

I remember being impressed with the fact that your father kept a Greek Testament in his seat in Church and always followed the lessons in it. It was at this time that he presented me with a copy of the first book of verse that Yeats ever published, *The Wanderings of Oisin.* I knew Yeats slightly and was greatly impressed by the emphatic way in which your father said that he would one day be a great poet. I could not myself detect much sign of greatness in that early volume, but I took your father's word for it.

I think he must have left Delgany in 1890 or 1891. I fix the date in this way. My own first attempt at writing was made in 1891 or early 1892. It was a short story and I *sent* it, not *took* it, to your father for criticism and advice. If he had been at Delgany I should have taken it to him, so he must have been somewhere else. His letter in reply was very encouraging and he advised me to send the story to ' Temple Bar ', which I did and it was published early in 1893. That gets us somewhere near the date of his leaving Delgany. I did shortly afterwards write a short one-Act play which was also sent to your father ; again he was most encouraging but was of the opinion that the interest of the play was too purely local to allow of any chance of its being produced.

After that I lost sight of your father, although he must have been living no farther off than Dublin.[4] In 1905 I came in touch with him again when I published my first novel, *The Seething Pot.* This was published anonymously,[5] and for a little while the secret was kept. Your father was one of the first to discover it. I met him one day in Stephen's Green, outside the University Club. He stopped me and began to talk about *The Seething Pot,* and to draw certain deductions from the book itself as to the authorship. I suppose my manner was nervous and embarrassed for he suddenly said to me, ' Did you write it ? ' I confessed, although I had fully made up my mind to lie about it if asked a direct question. He

[1] It was in 1886.

[2] The house was called ' Fairview '.

[3] He was Rolleston's brother-in-law and became afterwards Librarian of Trinity College, Dublin.

[4] Actually he was in London in 1892 and 1893 and in Killiney from 1893 to 1896 ; then Dublin.

[5] As by ' George A. Birmingham '.

then wrote a very favourable account of the book in a little publication called *Dana*. I believe, though I am not quite certain about this, that he also wrote about the book to Charles Graves, then Assistant Editor of the *Spectator*. This resulted in a long and very appreciative review in the *Spectator*, and was the beginning of such reputation and success as the book had. If I'm right about this I owe it all to your father.

Shortly afterwards he asked me to lunch with him at Jammet's and there I met Dr. Sigerson and some well-known English man of letters, whose name I have unfortunately totally forgotten. It was my first introduction to anything that could be called Literary Society, and I remember being very shy and tongue-tied, and your father being extremely kind.

My daughter and I have just gone over some old files of letters and I have found four from your father which I am sending you, but I would very much like to have them returned. The earliest in date refers to the incident in Stephen's Green about which I have just told you.

One of Rolleston's letters enclosed with this illustrates very well two of my father's outstanding characteristics—his candour and his honesty. Most of his work for various newspapers and reviews lay in the field of criticism and was the more valuable because he always said and wrote exactly what he thought without respect for persons. In view of his deep desire to see Irish literature achieve the greatness of which he thought it capable and of which the material it had to work on made it worthy, he might have been expected to write sometimes more kindly than his real opinion suggested he should. He would not do this, however ; if he thought anything blameworthy he spoke his mind about it, despite the fact that the writer whose work was under review might be a great personal friend. Rolleston was no log-roller. Unfortunately I have not been able to find any of his notices of *The Seething Pot*, but he made no bones about telling Hannay personally what he thought of the latter's picture of George Moore.

The beginning of this letter, incidentally, discloses a certain amount of innocent deception. My stepmother tells me that he had already come to the conclusion that Hannay had written *The Seething Pot* before meeting him in St. Stephen's Green and having his suspicions verified.

104 PEMBROKE ROAD,
MARCH 9TH, 1905   DUBLIN.
MY DEAR HANNAY,

When I got your letter to-night I was just about to write to apologise to you for my inexcusable indiscretion in asking you about the book. The fact is I was taken by surprise too. I never imagined it could be anyone living at a distance from Dublin and its literary circle.[1] You'd be quite right in denying authorship and rest assured that no one shall learn it through me—or even that I know the secret.

I feel extremely proud to have had anything to do, however remotely, with the production of such a book. What I think of it you will learn from my letter in the New York *Evening Post*, which I sent off last night—the ' best paper in America ', as a very good judge has described it to me. I'll send you a copy. I think also of reviewing it in *Dana*. I have been telling various booksellers to get it and push it, and have put it down for the Royal Dublin Society's Library.

But I must frankly say that I cannot approve of one feature in it—the portrait of George Moore. Moore's *Untilled Field* is the only book I would think of putting beside it as one of the *essential* books to read about modern Irish life. I think when you wish to paint a character so objectionable as Dennis Browne ultimately becomes in your book you should take pains not to give details like the omelet story, etc., which identify your victim so plainly. Nor do I think your appreciation of him at all just. Moore is not a reptile, in spite of his veneer of Nietzscheism, but an artist of true genius and a man of sincere convictions which he would rather starve than belie. Of course you didn't know Moore ; you painted the impression which newspaper-talk about him gave you—but it's like Dickens and Leigh Hunt ; Dickens didn't mean to paint Hunt as Harold Skimpole, but he endowed Skimpole with unmistakable traits of Hunt and did a grave injustice to Hunt in the circle where Hunt was known. Moore won't suffer, for he is better able to take care of himself than poor Hunt was ; but your book will, for people whose opinion you would value will feel, as I said in my American article, that your portrayal of Dennis Browne belongs properly to the region of polemic, not of literature.

There are a thousand things I want to say and talk over in reference to this book and I hope I'll have an opportunity of doing so with you some day. You have crystallised an epoch of Irish history in it, and in such a way that we must all turn with new interest to watch the next move in the great

[1] Hannay was then Rector of Westport, Co. Mayo.

game. I'm inclined to agree with O'Hara—if we only had a King ! A real King, not one of those stodgy Guelphs.[1] But if he doesn't come soon there'll be nothing left in Ireland, as Moore says, but the ox and the priest.

Ever yours sincerely and gratefully,

T. W. ROLLESTON

Later Hannay, whose friendship my father valued very highly, sent him the manuscript of *Hyacinth* to look through and on its publication Rolleston wrote to him as follows in February 1906 :

Hyacinth came all right, and I have sent my review of it to the New York paper. It was a very poor review. I am sorry. I was out of the mood, and it was American mail day, and when I had written the thing I knew I ought to have torn it up and re-written it, but I let it go ; the fact of it being mail day seemed like fate and I had no will. Indigestion, I suppose. I don't mean, by the way, that I slated the book, but I wrote poor, external, uncritical kinds of things. It was all that would come just then. Try and forgive me. I did enjoy the book extremely. You have made few if any changes, but it certainly goes better in print than it seemed to me to do in MS. The crucial scene with the Rev. Beecher when Hyacinth's mind is turned seems to me to stand out more clear and strong, and Maria to mean something more than had appeared to me before. Of course there are faults of want of unity, the point of interest shifting too frequently ; and of the story being a variation on the same theme as *The Seething Pot* which latter I still think a finer work. But anyway *Hyacinth* is something we must all be grateful to you for ; which means of course that you will be nearly as much abused for it as Sir Horace Plunkett for his ' Ireland '.[2] I see the *Independent* has opened fire to-day. I shouldn't be surprised if that blackguard . . . tries to do so in a more or less literal sense some time. Augusta ought to be grateful ; you've made her a much more interesting person than she is.

' Augusta ' was the famous Maud Gonne, the very handsome daughter of an English mother and a father who, though Irish, was an officer in the British Army ; in spite of her parentage she was at that time one of the most irreconcilably anti-English people in Ireland. She was a familiar figure in Dublin when she drove through the streets in her own outside-car always accompanied by a huge Irish wolf-hound.

[1] See page 163.
[2] *Ireland in the New Century*, by the Right Hon. Sir Horace Plunkett, K.C.V.O., F.R.S., published by John Murray, 1904.

By the end of the 'nineties the Irish Literary Revival was an accomplished fact ; a literature had been created, and was being added to almost daily, which had put a new and glorious wing to the cultural edifice which these islands of ours have built through the centuries. Ireland began the structure in her own language many centuries ago and Ireland completed it in the English language in the closing years of the nineteenth century. The knowledge that my father, T. W. Rolleston, was the real architect of the structure's Irish wing will ever be one of my proudest possessions.

On his death in 1920 the Editor of the *Irish Book Lover* wrote of him :

The Grim Reaper has been busy of late, and all too frequently have I had to deplore the passing of some friend or contributor, but not one whose loss I feel more than that of T. W. Rolleston. Some people found him distant and reserved, but that, I think, was the natural modesty of the man. I am free to confess that my experience of his friendship for nigh upon thirty years was quite the reverse ; he was always kind, genial, and ever helpful ; one of Nature's noblemen. His long services to the Irish Literary Society can never be forgotten. He was pressed more than once to accept the Presidency, but his modesty held him back, though no one deserved the honour more. I remember once hearing Sir Charles Gavan Duffy, in reference to the Society's success, apply the lines of Samuel Ferguson slightly altered : ' Under God to T. W. Rolleston, Does the greater praise belong.'

II

POLITICAL AND INDUSTRIAL

LONG before the deposition in 1890 and death in 1891 of Charles Stewart Parnell many Irishmen who desired Home Rule but did not regard continued hatred of England as a necessary concomitant had despaired of their country making any progress towards the desired end—or indeed towards any worth-while end at all—under the leadership of its politicians. The following, for example, is copied from a pamphlet issued in 1886, the authorship of which I have not been able to establish. It reads like T. W. Rolleston, but can hardly have been his seeing that the copy in my possession was sent or given to him by his brother-in-law, Henry Truell. It is called ' Union or Separation ' and was apparently fathered by the ' Irish Loyal and Patriotic Union ' ; towards the end this sentence occurs :

An Irish Parliament will be composed of the same elements as are found among the Irish Members now gathered under the banner unfurled by Mr. Parnell ; only its members will be more numerous, more hostile to the friends of England, more unscrupulous—if that be possible—and more rapacious, less restrained by decency or prudence than they are now.

Many ardent Home Rulers, among them T. W. Rolleston, held such opinions as these of the Irish Members and no student of the history of Ireland at that time could blame them. But, before passing on to another phase of Rolleston's work, I think it may be of interest to sketch in some of the factors that have created the undying ' Irish Question ' and to say something about the Rolleston family's position in the country.

As already stated we first went to Ireland in the reign of James I, from whom we received a grant of land in County Armagh. We have always therefore been Sassenachs and land-lords, and were—and are—Protestants into the bargain. Yet

42

despite these attributes—sufficient to damn any other non-Irish family—neither we nor our lands nor property have ever been even threatened with the fate suffered by so many other families in Ireland. As 'landed gentry' we should have been a fair target for the cattle-drivers and maimers, for United Irish Leaguers on the war-path, and for the other pestilential plagues from which Ireland to her sorrow has suffered almost continuously.

Why was this? I suppose the normal answer would be that we were good landlords, that we gave our tenants a square deal, that if crops failed in a bad season we rebated rents—which were never on an unjustly high scale—and above all that we were not absentees. The 'absentee landlord' who lived in luxury in England—or was at any rate believed to do so—on rents extracted, harshly if need be, from impoverished Irish tenants by agents for whom strong police guards had constantly to be provided, has been one of the major curses of Ireland. The agent's sole job was to collect rents by every means in his power and to evict, under the protection of the law, tenants who did not pay, whether non-payment arose from disinclination or sheer inability; the reason mattered not. 'No money? All right—out you go', even though the potatoes might be lying at the cottage door stricken black and foul with the blight.

But there were many other landlords besides ourselves who were not absentees, who treated their tenants every bit as well as we did, but yet who did not escape the tyrannies and brutalities of the United Irish Leaguers when a wave of anti-grazing fury swept over Ireland shortly before the war. In those times the fact that an individual had always behaved with normal decency to his tenants was not enough and did not win him the favour of the cattle-drivers; if he used his land for grazing, which gives little employment, he became a victim of men whose brutalities were not confined to the landlord's stock but extended also to himself, his family, and his property. Why then were the Rollestons exempt? Here is the story.

At the height of the anti-grazing agitation one of my cousins was riding her horse along a country road not far from the village of Shinrone in King's County and about a mile and a half or two miles from Glasshouse, where my branch of the family had lived for many years. Hilda, the cousin in question,

—she is now Mrs. Dalrymple—was stopped by some United Irish Leaguers who were strangers to that particular district, was made to dismount, being obviously of the landlord class, and might have been seriously molested had not some local members of the League appeared on the scene. They put things to rights at once, apologised profusely, and told the non-local men to clear out. After that they helped Hilda to remount and saw her safely on her way home.

Next day my uncle, Hilda's father, was a bit alarmed to see a small body of men coming up the drive at Glasshouse. Naturally he thought his turn had come to be dealt with by the Leaguers but agreed at once to see the men when they asked for him. Instead, however, of the anticipated demands regarding his land he found the atmosphere quite friendly and over a glass of whiskey in the dining-room he was presented with a document signed by the leaders of the local branch of the United Irish League in which he was given *carte blanche* to do with his land what he pleased and to come and go, himself and his family, without fear of molestation. The deputation, for such it was, also apologised again for the indignity Hilda had been made to suffer the previous day.

Somewhat mystified my uncle asked why a Sassenach landlord and a Protestant should be singled out for such an extraordinary concession, granted probably to no one else of his kind in Ireland. The astonishing answer was, in effect, ' Shure, we haven't forgotten what your Honour's father did for Mike Flanagan '.

The fact was that these incomprehensible people had remembered something my grandfather, the Judge, had done for one of his tenants fifty or more years earlier. There had been a murder and the tenant in question, against whom there was a great deal of circumstantial evidence, was arrested, charged with the crime, and committed for trial. I have called him ' Mike Flanagan ' because I don't know what his name really was, and it was as likely to have been Mike Flanagan as anything else.

Now my grandfather, Charles Rolleston-Spunner, did not believe Mike was guilty and, being then a Barrister, undertook his defence, a thing which anyone else in similar circumstances and with a spark of decency would have done too. Fees for the defence were, of course, out of the question ;

had all the tenants on the property clubbed together they could not have paid any.

The trial duly took place ; my grandfather did his best but without success ; the evidence against the man was too strong and Mike was hanged. Many years afterwards, however, he was exonerated by a confession made to the priest by the real murderer when he was dying.

It was this episode that the Leaguers referred to when they said, ' Shure, we haven't forgotten what your Honour's father did for Mike Flanagan '.

What can one do with such a people ? They don't react to any of the ordinary rules of conduct ; at the time in question practically every landlord was anathema for the simple reason perhaps that he *was* a landlord, but yet the sentiment attaching to an incident that had taken place half a century before was allowed to overshadow all other considerations and to compel the Leaguers to act in a manner utterly at variance with their whole plan of campaign—a plan which, where other landlords were concerned, was put into effect with rigour and brutality.

On the other hand may not the incident suggest that there is a key with which the Irish problem may be solved ? It is always the appeal to sentiment that will sway the people of Ireland ; I say ' the people of Ireland ' rather than ' the Irish people ' because those like ourselves, who have been in the country for more than three hundred years, have acquired this characteristic in quite as full measure as the Irish themselves. My countrymen set no store whatever by expediency, logic, money, business advantages, or any of the other considerations that would shape the conduct of an Englishman in any given circumstances. But pull an Irishman's heart-strings and he will follow you to Hades—priest or no priest—if you ask him to.

It is for this reason that one seldom hears of a wealthy Irishman ; the business magnate who has amassed a large fortune is unknown in the South ; if there is a rich man in the country outside Ulster it may be taken for granted that his wealth will have come not from business dealings but from the land or from a calling or profession with an heroic, emotional, or sentimental appeal. And the accumulation of riches will also probably have been an accident ; it will not have been for the purpose of making money that an Irishman will have embarked on or persevered in the particular occupation he has chosen.

The callings that appeal to the Irishman are the Army, the Church—particularly the Roman Catholic Church with its appeals to the emotions—the Police, Literature, Doctoring and Surgery, and less often the Navy. None of these professions is ordinarily calculated to lead to riches, but on the other hand, they are all callings which have honourable and often heroic traditions and provide the background for tales and legends whose appeal is to the heart rather than the head. In literature the Irish man and woman finds a medium not perhaps so much for personal achievement as for enshrining and glorifying the deeds of others—for doing in fact vicariously what chance or circumstances may prevent the individual from doing or attempting personally.

In Ireland sentiment takes the place occupied in the English make-up by material interests, and it is perfectly useless for the Englishman or his Government to expect lasting results from the application to Irish problems of the rules or principles which might be successful in dealing with other races or nations—within or without the British Empire.

My father used to tell with great sadness a story which demonstrates very well how opportunities can be missed by England's failure to realise that in dealing with Ireland such weapons as tariffs and soldiers and subsidies and statements of economic advantages are just so much rubbish. It will be remembered that when the Great War broke out Ireland was on the verge of a Civil War of her own ; North and South were ready to fly at one another's throats, F. E. Smith was galloping over Ulster roads, and Sir Edward Carson was thundering over Ulster audiences. Then Germany intervened and did so moreover in a way that, while it stirred English people to horror by its ruthless stupidity, made on Ireland an impression ten times more telling. The Irish saw in the invasion of Belgium a threat to the freedom of another small nation like themselves ; they saw also their old friend and ally, France, menaced by her powerful neighbour ; and they visualised the war being fought to a conclusion, as it was, on the same territory—the ' Cockpit of Europe '—where in times past the Irish Brigade had fought so gallantly side by side with Ireland's Gallic friends.

Why not, they said, form a new Irish Brigade, to fight again on the same ground as before and for the same French cause but this time not against England but with her? Can one not see how such an appeal would have affected the Irish people? The pending Civil War instantly passed into history as the war that was never fought. John Redmond went post-haste to London and saw Mr. Asquith. 'May I,' he said, ' recruit for a new Irish Brigade to fight the Germans?' Asquith consulted Kitchener who, though born in County Kerry, was actually an Englishman, had spent a lifetime in the British Army, and had presumably lost, in the Staff College and the Military Drill Book, any sense of imagination his Irish birth might have given him. He said ' No, the risk is too great.' Asquith saw Redmond again and repeated ' No, the risk is too great; the Irish Regiments will be brigaded with English and Scottish Regiments.' He might as well have said straight out ' We do not trust you.'

Of course judged by English standards of measurement both Asquith and Kitchener were perfectly right; they saw in the then ' rebellious ' condition of Southern Ireland what was an obvious and grave risk and gave their decisions accordingly. A better appreciation, even an elementary knowledge of the Irish character and temperament and of the workings of the Irish mind would have told these Englishmen that the mere fact that they were prepared to take the risk would have removed the danger entirely. The emotions that would have been aroused by the re-forming of the Irish Brigade would have swept every man and boy in Ireland into the British Army; the trouble would have been to keep them out, not, as was actually the case, to get them in. There would have been no Easter ' Rebellion ' and the Irish question would have died and been buried on the Western Front.

As it was, a golden opportunity of making an irresistible appeal to Irish sentiment and emotions was lost. Though Kitchener's ruling was not strictly adhered to, permission was refused for the Southern Irish Divisions to carry the harp on their colours, though the Northern Division was permitted to use the Red Hand of Ulster! Is it any wonder that, in face of such ineptitude, Irish pre-war bitterness and hostility were kept alive or that later on the situation was such that conscription could not be made to apply to Ireland?

But why, in these circumstances, should Ireland have been deliberately placed in a different position from England with regard to such questions as compensation for damage caused to land and property which had been commandeered for military purposes? The British Government could and did appropriate Irish land for such purposes as the construction of aerodromes and the establishment of camps, but not one penny of compensation was given to the dispossessed owners either at the time or later, when the land was handed back almost ruined for agricultural or grazing purposes. The Irish people were specifically excluded by Act of Parliament from the receipt of any such compensation, though it was paid liberally on the other side of the Irish Sea. Why? Because forsooth Ireland would not be conscripted. That is not a fair statement of the case; the Irish had offered to conscript themselves at the beginning of the war in the most effective way possible, but the offer was rejected. England could have turned every soul in Ireland into a willing—an enthusiastic—volunteer had Asquith and Kitchener only allowed them to join up in their own way as members of an Irish Brigade.

Here is an actual instance of what was taking place; I take it from an article of my father's which appeared in the *Nineteenth Century* for August, 1920:

In the winter of 1918, after the Armistice, the War Office returned to a landowner in County Dublin certain lands which had been compulsorily taken from her for public purposes. When returned they were found to have been very seriously deteriorated, to the extent, as sworn by a valuer, of £2,500. The owner applied for compensation; it was refused; and she sued the War Office, the case coming before the Master of the Rolls on the 13th December. The War Office denied liability on the express ground that although, under the regulation by which the lands were seized, there was a statutory provision for compensation, the provision applied to Great Britain alone. 'It was expressly provided', said Serjeant Matheson, Counsel for the War Office, 'that this was not to apply to Ireland. The plaintiff therefore learned, and all Ireland with her, that, although she as a taxpayer and citizen must pay her share of compensation to an English farmer whose lands were commandeered, there was no reciprocal obligation—the War Office might take her lands by force, treat them as it pleased, and deny all liability on the simple ground that she lived on the wrong side of St. George's Channel.

This sort of thing was nobody's fault? It couldn't have been helped? I say it was England's fault. If a country such as England undertakes to provide for the government of another country it is her business to find out how to do it, to ascertain to what beliefs and ideals the people to be governed subscribe, and to act accordingly. The most obscure and backward native race in Africa, the Pacific Islands, or New Guinea is ruled in this way, through its own chiefs and with the minimum amount of disturbance of tribal customs. Why not Ireland ? By all that is sane and logical why not Ireland ?

' Home Rule ' was, in the eyes of the vast majority of the Irish people—encouraged by their politicians—the one solution for all their troubles, but here the great stumbling-block was the intractability of the North. Ulster was, and is, comparatively prosperous, and in the shipbuilding yards of Belfast and the linen industry alone the Northern Counties possessed sources of wealth which the rest of Ireland could not hope to have. The people of the North, differing from the Southern Irish in temperament and often in religion, objected to any part of their wealth being used for the betterment of the South and it was known that if Home Rule were to materialise England would have to coerce Ulster into throwing in her lot with her less fortunate fellow-countrymen and into joining, as a minority, in governing the country through a Parliament in Dublin which must, on a population basis, be predominantly Southern and Roman Catholic.

Gladstone's First Home Rule Bill in 1886, had it passed, would have undoubtedly been followed, or possibly preceded, by an Irish Civil War ; but, on its defeat in the House of Commons, it was again rejected by the constituencies at a General Election.

The Second Home Rule Bill in 1893 passed the House of Commons mainly because various sections of the House wished to keep on the right side of the Prime Minister—Gladstone again—for purposes of their own which had nothing whatever to do with Ireland. However, the House of Lords rejected the Bill and Gladstone, then 83 years of age, gave up the struggle. Had this not happened and had any attempt been made to put Home Rule into operation the North would have revolted as in fact it did revolt in 1914, and as it has more recently—in January, 1938—expressed its intention

5

of doing again if any alteration is made in the position of Ulster.

Quite apart from many provisions which were objectionable or unworkable in all three of these measures there was one very good reason for both English and Northern Irish opposition to Home Rule. The political leaders of Southern Ireland were not at that time regarded as the kind of men to whom the responsibilities of government could be entrusted. It is a fact too that the type of man who has often come to the front in a political sphere has been of the worst type of the genus politician. The Irish are easily swayed by rhetoric and by appeals to the emotions ; sound arguments have nothing like the effect they should have and stand little chance of influencing an Irish election unless accompanied by strong emotional appeals. This of course is a defect in all electoral systems which permit speech-making in support of a cause or a party or an individual. The rhetorician, the ' tub-thumper ', the soap-box orator stands a far better chance of being elected than the man in whom possession of sound judgment is not allied with rhetorical powers and with that nimbleness of mind which enables him to score on the platform. In England the people are better fitted temperamentally to distinguish the chaff from the grain, but where Ireland was concerned the system put into the Parliament of the United Kingdom men whose qualifications to govern consisted almost solely of the ability to make moving speeches and to stir up passions. They were politicians and politicians only ; they inspired no confidence among people who really had the best interests of both North and South honestly at heart.

To these men, among whom were T. W. Rolleston, Horace Plunkett, George Russell, George Moore, Douglas Hyde, and many others, politics had little appeal ; they seemed a dirty business, as indeed they often are, and they chose to work for Ireland in other and less spectacular ways. Parnell they had regarded as possessing some of the qualities desirable in an Irish Prime Minister, but he and Gladstone failed to bring about Home Rule because the English people and Parliament were not prepared to coerce Ulster. They should not have tried to do so in 1914.

But Parnell's successors inspired no sort of confidence whatever ; all they did inspire in fact was the utmost repugnance.

Witness this letter written by Rolleston in about 1890 to Dr. Douglas Hyde, the founder of the Gaelic League ; it is dated from 16 Upper Mallow Street, Limerick :

MY DEAR HYDE,

I am here superintending the Intermediate Exam. at the Sacred Heart College and your letter was forwarded to me from Delgany. When I get home, which will be on the 22nd, I will look up an autograph of W.W.,[1] who, by the way, I see by to-day's ' Freeman ' is seriously ill and not likely to recover. He has done a big work in his time and one that will look bigger in a generation than it does now, except to a very few.

Since the publication of my pamphlet I have been more than ever convinced of the rightness of the view I took and of the publication of that view. I would rather wait ten years for Home Rule than let this damnable gang of swindlers and murderers continue to pose as Irish patriots without raising my voice against them. ' Landlord rapacity ! ' What on earth do you (? they) mean ? The laws, passed in the teeth of the Parnellites, absolutely prevent any return of the old tyrannical methods of landlordism, which, too, was never so bad, or so widely prevalent, as people now make out. The real trouble at present is largely that in the good times when tenants had a splendid surplus over their rents they launched out into wasteful and absurd expenditure instead of laying by for a rainy day. I don't see why the landlords should be punished for that. What, for instance, has Lord Clanricarde done ? His rents were absurdly low ; two years ago there was not a sixpence of arrears on the whole property ; the tenants dared not go into Court for they knew well the rents would be raised. I think he is perfectly right to exact them and to evict the whole district if the tenants, who are well able to pay, are foolish and dishonest enough not to do so.

I don't mind being praised by the *Spectator*. It has always written with great sympathy and understanding of Ireland and Irishmen, and is only *provisionally* anti-Nationalist. If I were an Englishman I should certainly be anti-Nationalist at present, or at least anti-League.

Ever yours,

T.W.R.

[1] Walt Whitman, the American poet.

The pamphlet referred to was published in 1888 and was entitled ' Boycotting ', being a reply to another with the same title published by Mr. S. Laing, a former Financial Secretary of the Treasury, Finance Minister of India, and Member of Parliament for Orkney and Shetland.   Rolleston's opinion of the Irish politician is stated therein only a little more mildly than in his letter to Douglas Hyde :

> Some Irishmen there certainly are whose dearest wish is to see just laws made for their country by its own National Government, and yet who hold that such laws never can be made, nor uprightly administered, by the representatives of a people trained to think that lying, bullying, plunder, and murder are proper weapons of political warfare.

Lord Clanricarde, whose estates were in Galway near Portumna on Lough Derg, was regarded as the worst of all Irish landlords ; he was also an absentee.   Rolleston, however, in whom a sense of fairness was an outstanding characteristic, did not think he was as bad as he was painted.   Clanricarde, whose name was de Burgh Canning, was the head of my mother's, the de Burgh, family ; his wealth was left to his nephew, the present Earl of Harewood, husband of the Princess Royal.

The ' League ' referred to was the United Irish League, an actively anti-English organisation, the successor of ' Young Ireland ' of the 1840's and of the Fenians of a later date.

That Rolleston's opinion of the Irish brand of politician did not alter in after years is shown by these further extracts from letters written to Canon Hannay :

> 12th March, 1905.   No doubt you noticed the extraordinary collapse of the political movement of to-day when the Bishops compelled the M.P's to go to Westminster, and keep a Tory and coercion Government in office in order to get a little State assistance for English Catholic schools !   It is simply laughable, after that, to think of such a party achieving Ireland's liberation in the House of Commons.   I regard that event as the real exit of Parliamentary politics from the Irish stage ; politics in fact have now been, like everything else, absorbed into the Church—everything else but *one* thing, and that one thing is the Gaelic League.   The League represents the last effort of the Irish spirit for nationality and a personal independence.   The Church began by opposing it ; it's now, as usual, doing its utmost to absorb it, when it will become a mere tame cat like the political party and cease to have any vital existence for the future of Ireland. Whether the League can resist the Church any better than the politicians did is very doubtful, but we must fight the matter out as best we can— and *qui vivra verra.*

The Gaelic League, which Rolleston was active in assisting Douglas Hyde and Miss Eleanor Hull to found, started its life at about the same time as the Irish Literary Society and was to some extent designed to run on parallel lines, though on a different plane. The I.L.S. was for the writers and playwrights, while the Gaelic League was for everyone to join who cared to do so. Its objects were to revive the Irish language per medium of classes wherever they could be got going and to direct the thoughts of its members towards the worth-while things in Irish history and mythology. Douglas Hyde was at that time doing magnificent work in committing to writing the old tales, many of which he took down for the first time from the lips of the West of Ireland peasants.

The Gaelic League was entirely non-political and non-sectarian, though, as Rolleston wrote in a letter to the Press in 1902, 'To be non-political does not mean that the League is to have no political views in matters that directly concern its existence and its work.' That, of course, could be said of any organisation and simply meant that, if political influence was to be used to prevent the League from trying to educate the Irish people into being more Irish, then the League would, *ipso facto*, become in that respect political.

Both the Church of Ireland (Protestant) and the Roman Catholic Church seem to have regarded the League with suspicion. This is reflected in a letter of Rolleston's to Canon Hannay in 1906, when we were living at Glenealy in County Wicklow :

We've just started a Gaelic Branch in Glenealy. They want me to be President of it. I don't know if it's constitutional to be President of two branches at once. I told them to get the P.P.[1] They say it's all they can do to keep him from denouncing them at the altar. They are only tolerated at all on condition that no girls are allowed to attend classes.

Then, after a reference to the *Church of Ireland Gazette*, which was about to print a lecture of Hannay's,

We are getting quite a lot of propagandist work into that organ, it seems. I wonder if we are affecting any minds among its readers ! I haven't heard or seen any evidence of it, though young clergymen sometimes say they would like to join the Gaelic movement, but don't dare to.

The Gaelic League, a perfectly harmless organisation,

[1] Parish Priest.

struggled on in spite of misrepresentations, but was eventually overcome by politics and became the ' tame cat ' that Rolleston feared it might.   The power of the Roman Catholic Church in a country where the mass of the people were unable to read or write and were forced to go to the Parish Priest for their opinions and for permission to do almost anything, was enormous.   But the League had done good work and doubtless many of those who now speak their native language fluently owe that accomplishment to the activities of an organisation which Douglas Hyde, in the dedication of his *Literary History of Ireland*, described as ' The only body in Ireland which appears to realise the fact that Ireland has a past, has a history, has a literature, and the only body in Ireland which seeks to render the present a rational continuation of the past.'

The Gaelic League was only one method, and a subsidiary one, whereby Rolleston and his associates hoped to liberate Ireland from the shackles of her past unfortunate history and to lift the people out of the poverty-stricken condition in which thousands of them barely existed, and from which they sometimes died.   They knew that the Irish question was not fundamentally a religious one and that there was in fact probably a greater degree of religious toleration in the South than in Presbyterian Ulster.   The question was primarily a land one, having its roots far back in Stuart and Cromwellian times.   It happened that, as the landlords were so many of them English or of English descent, the tenants and peasants, who were almost wholly Roman Catholic, in becoming anti-English became also anti-Protestant and were blind to every benefit that English rule and membership of the British Empire could, and often did, confer on their country.   This ranged the South against the ' loyalist ' North, where shipbuilding and the manufacture of linen had prospered under shrewd Scottish management and had led to financial prosperity and a firm attachment to England and the Empire wherein lay Ulster's best markets.   The Northerners did not want their consequent wealth to be taxed by a Dublin Parliament to provide public services, education, and so forth for a ' disloyal ' South whose population also subscribed to a religion which, rightly or wrongly, the North detested.   Money in fact was at the root of the Irish question as far as the differences be-

tween Ulster and the South were concerned. Others matters
are, and, properly handled, always have been, capable of
adjustment, but, while the South said in effect that money
belonging to any part of Ireland should be used for the benefit
of the country as a whole, the North replied that money made
in one corner belonged only to that corner. This attitude,
which has the appearance at any rate of selfishness, is still
persisted in, though it is generally hidden behind professions,
no doubt perfectly genuine in themselves, of loyalty, allegiance
to the Crown, and so forth. I quote the following letter
which appeared in the *Daily Telegraph* and *Morning Post* of
2nd February, 1938 on the eve of Ulster's ' No Coercion '
General Election. It appeared over the signature of Mr.
William Grant, a Member of the Northern Ireland Parliament :

> I have no desire to enter into a controversy with Dr. Nicholas Mansergh,
> for it is quite evident that he is against Lord Craigavon and the Ulster
> Government. But I should like to put two questions which are of vital
> importance :
> (1) Does he assert that the Ulster loyalists are wrong when they declare
> that under no circumstances will they give up their British citizenship
> within the United Kingdom ? and
> (2) Does he hold that they are foolish in not joining with Mr. de Valera
> in an all-Ireland Republic that owes no allegiance to His Majesty the King ?
> We in Ulster did not create partition. It was the Republicans who
> cut adrift from Great Britain, and now that things have not come up to
> expectations they want to rope in all Ulster.
> The external trade of Northern Ireland amounts to about £99,000,000
> per annum, as against £57,000,000 for the Free State. I wonder if this
> trading wealth is the attraction ?

The first part of this letter is just typical window-dressing ;
the real meat is in the last paragraph, though one is justified
in asking whether it is the South that is being greedy and
envious or the North that is being selfish in declining to
share its luscious financial bone with its hungry fellow-
countrymen.

This has always been the crux of the matter and, were
Southern Ireland as prosperous as the North, there is little
doubt that the latter would be clamouring to be allowed to
share in the good things.

How then could the Irish question be solved ? Obviously,
thought Rolleston and others—when they had despaired of the
Irish Members at Westminster setting about the job in the

right way—by making the South as financially prosperous as Ulster.   Hence in 1893 and 1894 we find such organisations coming into existence as the Irish Industries Association, the Irish Arts and Crafts Society, the Irish Agricultural Organisation Society, and, in 1899, at the urgent insistence of ' all the leading agricultural and industrial interests in the country'[1], the Department of Agriculture and Technical Instruction.

The immediate object of these movements was to increase the prosperity of the country by encouraging such industries as could be profitably carried on.   Beyond that desirable and commendable purpose was the realisation that, if the result were to be a diminution of the disparity between the wealth of the North and the poverty of the South, an immense obstacle to Home Rule for the whole country would have been removed.

But what a task confronted the men and women who sought in this way to deserve well of their country !   There was so little on which to build and there was such an endless road to travel, and they were faced with almost every conceivable handicap—in the industrial field at any rate if not the agricultural.   Irish industry had never had a chance of developing ; prior to the machine age restrictive legislation had wellnigh strangled the country in the interests of English and Colonial businesses, and when the Industrial Revolution arrived Ireland found herself without any of the natural advantages which enabled England to take such successful advantage of the new methods and new opportunities.   Ireland had no coal, no iron, no raw materials worth mentioning, and no capital with which to erect factories wherein to use raw materials that might perhaps have been imported.

English products had up till then been made by the people in their own homes, looms for cloth-making being sometimes hired out to them by their owners—capitalists—who bought back the resultant product.   After the Revolution all this changed and the factory system with its enormously increased output took the place in England of the home-and-cottage arrangement.   Not so in Ireland, however, where only a few home industries, catering for little more than local requirements, managed to survive.   Agriculture and farming pro-

[1] *Ireland in the New Century*, by Sir Horace Plunkett, p. 223.

vided the people with almost their sole means of livelihood, and the famine of 1846 almost completed the impoverishment of an already nearly destitute people :

The potato was blighted in every part of Ireland in July and August, 1846 ; it did not yield a twentieth part of its usual increase ; the crop of cereals too was excessively short ; the harvest in a word almost completely failed. The loss in money was estimated at sixteen millions sterling ; this may afford some idea of what the results were in a country already impoverished and always very poor. Even in the best and most prosperous districts, society was disorganised in a short time ; there was a general calling in of debts and demands ; the landed gentry received but a fraction of rent ; hundreds of farmers of the better class became bankrupt ; thousands of peasants fled from their homes in despair. In less fortunate counties the consequences were, of course, more grave ; but in the districts which had suffered the year before, and in all those which were more or less backward, the condition of affairs soon became appalling. Famine advanced slowly from the coastline, from Donegal southwards to Kerry and Cork, and, gradually making its way inland, threw its dark shadow over a third part of Ireland ; starving multitudes were lifted up from the land and tossed to and fro to seek the means of prolonging life ; and thousands sank into unknown graves.[1]

Another factor which contributed in no small degree to foster the perpetual unrest of Ireland was the fact that agriculture is a seasonal business ; for long periods every year no work can be done ; ploughing is impossible in winter because the ground is too hard ; and seed-sowing and harvesting have to be completed at definite times extending over comparatively short periods. At other seasons the agricultural worker is perforce idle and the Irish tenants and farm workers had in consequence many opportunities of meeting in the villages and elsewhere to discuss and keep alive their grievances against the hated English. Some of them even blamed her directly for the famine !

What the founders of the Irish Industries Association and kindred bodies wished to do in these difficult circumstances was to revive the home industries of the peasantry by introducing organisation, finding markets, and improving methods— as opportunity and finance permitted—gradually replacing hand-looms, spinning-wheels, and so forth with such machinery

---

[1] *Ireland from 1798 to 1898*, by William O'Connor Morris. A. D. Innes and Co., Ltd.

as could be installed in the people's own homes or perhaps in village or country centres when some degree of centralisation was necessary for profitable development.

The Irish Industries Association, to which the prefix ' Royal ' was subsequently added, was founded by the late Ishbel, Marchioness of Aberdeen and Temair, then the Countess of Aberdeen, in 1894.   T. W. Rolleston became Managing Director and Secretary and was responsible for bringing George W. Russell into the organisation as his first lieutenant.   Many people who only know of George Russell as ' AE ', the poet, are unaware that he was also a business man and accountant of high attainments and an organiser whose services to the I.I.A. and later to Sir Horace Plunkett's Irish Agricultural Organisation Society—the ' I.A.O.S.'—were quite invaluable. Before joining the Irish Industries Association he had been an accountant at Pim's, the big Dublin draper's shop.

Under Rolleston's guidance the Association did splendid work and achieved much by preserving from extinction many Irish handicrafts, particularly lace-making and the manufacture of those homespuns for which the country is famous. Rolleston spent much of his time travelling about the country, lecturing, encouraging, organising, and devising means of establishing industries suitable to each particular locality.

The results of this work, allied with that of the Arts and Crafts Society—of which Rolleston was also Honorary Secretary from 1898 to 1908—of the Congested Districts Board, which operated on somewhat similar lines, of the Irish Agricultural Organisation Society, and of the Department of Agriculture and Technical Instruction—where Rolleston was for five years Organiser of Lectures—could have been seen in the Home Industries Section of the Irish International Exhibition held in Dublin in 1907.   The range of manufactures shown thereat was amazing, more particularly when it is remembered that none of the innumerable products had been made in what could properly be called a ' factory '.   They included lace, crotchet work, homespuns, carpets, linen, damask, cambric, curtains, shirts, hosiery, boots, straw hats, gloves, art-metal work, wood carving, baskets, and a host of other products many of which had hitherto been imported.   In a foreword to a book on *Irish Rural Life and Industry*, published in connection with this Exhibition, Lady Aberdeen wrote :

Our great wish and hope is that by presenting a series of well-arranged and attractive exhibits produced by the skill of trained cottage workers who have been supplied with good designs, and who have been brought into touch with the demands of the market, visitors would be led to think of how much more could be done, and whether *they* could not help in the doing of it.

It is a pity that we could not have preserved the collection of Home Industries Exhibits sent to the International Exhibition at Edinburgh twenty-one years ago, to place alongside the goods we are now able to display, and thus to have illustrated the progress made, and to have encouraged those who have patiently worked in this movement during all the intervening years.

One would have thought that these movements, these first steps on a road designed to lead to some sort of industrial prosperity and to keep more Irish people occupied for longer periods of each year, would have been welcomed and assisted by all sections in the country. Such, however, was not the case ; the Nationalist politicians as a whole held rigidly aloof, fearing of course that their own prestige and influence would diminish if the leaders of an industrial revival were to be more favourably regarded than themselves ; and from other directions came more active opposition which was apparently ready to go to extreme lengths to prevent Irish industry from prospering. I take the following from my father's diary for 19 June 1897 :

Yesterday called by appointment on Miss S. Sturge at the London and North Western Railway Hotel, Northwall. She was on her way back to her basket industry at Letterfrack. She wanted to see me with a view to getting the industry taken off her hands, as she was subjected to a continual system of persecution . . . . . culminating in two attempts to murder her by poison. I told her she would have to go to America and find some members of a Celtic basket firm and get them to run the thing through a representative here.

The fact of course was that the uniting of Unionist and Nationalist under a banner of common—industrial—interests would inevitably have operated to reduce the influence of the politicians and of the Roman Catholic Church ; and the bringing together in this manner of the Unionist North and the Nationalist South would probably have led in the end to Home Rule for all Ireland without the assistance of the Irish Members.

Rolleston foreshadowed this result in a most interesting pamphlet published by him at his own expense in 1900 when the Boer War was in progress. This pamphlet, called ' Ireland, the Empire, and the War ', dealt mainly with Ireland's attitude and actions in relation to the hostilities in South Africa, but towards the end Rolleston referred in outline to the organisations which were really trying to do something for the country :

In recent times voluntary organisations have sprung up to make head against the denationalisation of Irish intellect and to promote the development of Irish capacity. There are the Gaelic League, the Feis Ceoil, the National Literary Society, the Irish Arts and Crafts Society, the Irish Literary Theatre, and, in the economic sphere, there is the Irish Agricultural Organisation Society. There is also a great deal of diffused unorganised force in what is called the Irish Literary Movement. These various movements and organisations are working under enormous difficulties. They are very much in the position of teachers trying to give an art education to pupils who have never learned drawing. But they are practically the sole fosterers and guardians of the national idea—of that without which all the Acts of Parliament that ever were written could not make Ireland a nation. And there is this very significant fact to be noted about them—that they are one and all founded on the non-political basis, one and all have set their doors wide to Home Ruler and Unionist alike, and do as a matter of fact receive unreserved sympathy and aid from both sources. These movements, therefore, which represent the true, genuine, and practical nationalism of the country run directly counter to the present trend of political nationalism, which no sooner sees anything like common action going on between Home Ruler and Unionist than it proclaims it as something to be denounced and smitten down. The nationalism of the spirit and the nationalism of contemporary party politics refuse to coalesce and harmonise. There are some weighty deductions to be drawn from that fact.

Considerations of this kind will lead us to the third and last principle I have to put forward—the encouragement of united action among Irishmen of all creeds, classes, and political camps in every sphere of action that admits of it. (There is a footnote here saying ' Which for the present cannot include the Parliamentary sphere '.) It is now clearly an idle dream to think that Home Rule can be ' rushed ' by one of the two sections that compose the Irish people against the determined and, on the whole, justified opposition of the other. I do not believe that the expectations that were raised by the pettifogging and impracticable Bills of Mr. Gladstone—measures which, if they had been passed, would have meant the swift ruin of this country—were ever at all so near realisation as they at one time seemed to be. The two Irish nations must first be made one before another frontal attack can have any chance of success. They must come together, as they are doing, in the work of intellectual and economic development—they must come together, as they will do if they are permitted, in the work of local government ; and out of their united action over the whole range of Irish internal interests will rise in the end a united demand, which will be granted as a matter of course, for greater power to promote those interests. It may not be out of place to point out that much has already been accomplished in this direction. It has been accomplished, exactly on the lines here described, by the Recess Committee.[1] The most significant and interesting fact about that body seems to have hitherto escaped public attention—it is that, while a political agitation had been demonstrating, agitating, cheering, voting, and what not, for Home Rule to no purpose whatever, Mr. Horace Plunkett, aided by a few Unionist and Nationalist friends, has been quietly putting it into practice—and not a hair of the Constitution has been ruffled ! And one can conceive that the principle of the Recess Committee, systematised, expanded, and sanctioned—as it easily might be—might develop into a form of Home Rule which would be a natural growth of the soil and thoroughly acceptable to all sections of our people. We should be guided aright in these matters if we clearly understood that each of the nations of Ireland has laid hold of one side of a great truth, but neither has yet grasped the whole. One of them clings to the conception of Ireland's place and power in the Empire—the other to the conception of her separate individuality and freedom. Both are right and both are wrong. Each of them has told a half-truth, complementary parts of the great ideal which shall yet give Ireland both world-power and freedom and make her a nation indeed. When that ideal shall receive open recognition and allegiance, the time will at last have come when the old political distinctions can be merged in what was once called ' a brotherhood of affection, a communion of rights, and a union of power ' among Irishmen of every class and creed.

That was written thirty-nine years ago. The Ulster Revolt, the Great War, the Easter Rising of 1916, the Partition of Ireland, the Treaty of 1921, de Valera's Constitution, and the Agreement of 1938 have intervened but every word of it is as true as when it was first published in 1900. Fundamentally the Irish position remains unchanged—as does the remedy.

The Irish Agricultural Organisation Society, more commonly and conveniently alluded to as the ' I.A.O.S.', was formed by Sir Horace Plunkett in 1894 in order to co-ordinate the activities of about a score of separate co-operative bodies which Plunkett himself had already been mainly instrumental in forming. The principles upon which this Society operated

---

[1] The Recess Committee was a gathering which sat in 1896 under the Presidency of Horace Plunkett, who initiated the step. It represented both political and business interests from both North and South and its object was to find a ' way out ' for Ireland on industrial lines. The reader is referred to Plunkett's *Ireland in the New Century*. The Committee derived its name from the fact that it sat during a Parliamentary Recess.

were broadly speaking those of the Co-operative movement
which originated in Manchester, though in actual application
the I.A.O.S. was concerned more with production than selling.
Plunkett thus sums up the need for such a movement in his
Ireland in the New Century :

> Generally speaking the task before us in Ireland was the adaptation to
> the special circumstances of our country of methods successfully pursued
> by communities similarly situated in foreign countries. We had to urge
> upon farmers that combination was just as necessary to their economic
> salvation as it was recognised to be by their own class, and by those engaged
> in other industries, elsewhere. They must combine, so we urged on them,
> for example, to buy their agricultural requirements at the cheapest rate
> and of the best quality in order to produce more efficiently and more
> economically ; they must combine to avail themselves of improved appli-
> ances beyond the reach of individual producers, whether it be by the
> erection of creameries, for which there was urgent need, or of cheese
> factories and jam factories which might come later ; or, in ordinary farm
> operations, to secure the use of the latest agricultural machinery and the
> most suitable pure-bred stock ; they must combine—not to abolish middle
> profits in distribution whether those of the carrying companies or those
> of the dealers in agricultural produce—but to keep those profits within
> reasonable limits, and to collect in bulk and regularise consignments so
> that they could be carried and marketed at a moderate cost ; they must
> combine, as we afterwards learned, for the purpose of creating, by mutual
> support, the credit required to bring in the fresh working capital which
> each new development of their industry would demand and justify. In
> short, whenever and wherever the individuals in a farming community
> could be brought to see that they might advantageously substitute associ-
> ated for isolated production or distribution, they must be taught to form
> themselves into associations in order to reap the anticipated advantages.

The I.A.O.S. was to run, and in fact did run, on parallel
lines to the Irish Industries Association, but operating in the
sphere of primary instead of secondary production. Its success
was most encouraging and by 1903 it had established 800
member societies representing 400,000 persons and with a
turnover of about £2,000,000 per annum.[1]

It will be noted that the I.A.O.S did not impinge in any
way on politics ; it was a purely business organisation ; but
for all that, Rolleston had to write, in a brief review of the
period, published in the *Observer* in 1917 :

> The Irish Nationalist representatives since the death of Parnell evidently
> regarded economic development in Ireland as something dangerous to
> nationality, as they conceived it—and they conceived it narrowly as a

---

[1] See also p. 65.

change in political machinery. They fought bitterly against the estab-
lishment of the Agricultural Department ; they fought, and are fighting
still, against agricultural co-operation ; at a time when they held the
Government at their mercy they permitted a handling of the Cunard
Company's contract [1] in a manner which is said to have cost the South of
Ireland £400,000 a year ; they insisted on the repeal of the Wyndham
Act on the sole ground that it was too successful ; they have done nothing
for the Irish school teachers, nothing to insist on Ireland getting her fair
share of munition work, nothing for the development of Ireland's magnificent harbours ; and they have not only ignored Ulster, but up to 1914
nothing could exceed the plainness with which they advertised the fact
that they did not want Ulster or any other kind of loyalists in the national
movement. If any British statesman showed a symptom of interest in
Ireland's well-being they jeered at him for trying to ' kill Home Rule
with kindness '. And the British statesmen, being human, and also much
harassed by importunities from every side, naturally followed the line of
least Parliamentary resistance. They saw that they would get no thanks
for anything they did for Ireland, and that they might as well save their
energy, and the nation's money, for more fruitful fields of reform. They
were wrong of course ; excessively and stupidly wrong ; but it is not just
that they alone should bear the blame for Ireland's failure to get her fair
share as a member of the United Kingdom.

Rolleston never made any secret of his opinion that political
Nationalism, as it flourished at all material times, would never
do Ireland much good. The Irish Members in consequence
did not like him or his friend, Sir Horace Plunkett. This
attitude is reflected in an incident in 1908 which created
somewhat of a sensation at the time and resulted in an open
attack by John Redmond and his henchman, John Dillon,
on the I.A.O.S., Plunkett, and Rolleston.

What happened was that a Mr. T. W. Russell—who must
on no account be confused with ' AE '—having succeeded
Plunkett as Vice-President of the (Irish) Department of Agriculture, had issued certain regulations which affected the
work of the I.A.O.S. Means had to be devised to overcome
the handicap imposed by these regulations, which put a time-
limit to public subventions to the I.A.O.S. Plunkett addressed
his organisation on the subject and said, amongst other things,
that it was inevitable that a political issue should be raised,
Russell, as head of a Government Department, having presumably acted on the suggestion of, or at any rate with the
approval of, the Irish Members, whose hostility to the I.A.O.S.
was notorious.

[1] To call at Queenstown.

As the Irish Home Rule cause had for a long time possessed a very large number of supporters in America, and as large sums of money crossed the Atlantic at various times to foster the anti-English movement, the Irish Members were naturally sensitive to any unfavourable opinions that might be expressed about them in the United States. Plunkett's address was printed and circulated and he suggested to Rolleston that he might care to send copies of it to some of his American and Irish-American friends. Rolleston readily agreed to do so and sent the address to, among others, a Mr. Edward Devoy of St. Louis whom he had known at the time of the St. Louis Exhibition in 1904 as a warm admirer of Plunkett and the work he was doing. John Redmond, however—though this is by the way—referred to Devoy as ' one of the best friends and supporters ' of his political party.

Rolleston naturally sent a covering letter to Devoy with the address and in it expressed some of his well-known opinions about the Irish Nationalist Parliamentarians. This was a purely private letter but Devoy does not seem to have appreciated that fact and published it. Then the storm broke. Redmond accused Plunkett of conspiring secretly against him with Rolleston's assistance, and John Dillon in the House of Commons said it was ' the intention of Sir Horace Plunkett to destroy the Irish Party and the Home Rule movement ', his argument being of course, as he had publicly stated a short time previously, that ' if the National cause is killed in America it will soon die in Ireland.' Both Redmond and Dillon said, without any but *prima facie* justification, that the ' Rolleston letter ', as it came to be called, was written at Plunkett's request and that its writer had for years been an official of the I.A.O.S., both of which statements were quite untrue ; Rolleston was never at any time in the service of the I.A.O.S. and hastened to state publicly both in Ireland and America that Plunkett had had nothing to do with his letter ; further, to refute Dillon's statement that he was attacking Home Rule, he quoted as follows from the letter itself :

No sort of attack on Home Rule or upon Home Rulers as such is dreamt of. It is merely insisted that Irish farmers shall not choose people who will use their power, as Dillon and the rest of the Parliamentarians have been doing, to crush the farmers' movement for the better organisation of his business.

No action for libel followed the publication of this damaging statement.

Plunkett and Rolleston were both themselves supporters of the principle of Home Rule for Ireland but they did not approve of the methods adopted by the Irish Members to attain it. But what Plunkett objected to mainly in the accusation of ' conspiracy ' that arose out of this matter was not so much the charge itself but the fact that, according to Dillon and Co., he was trying to engineer a *secret* campaign. During the newspaper correspondence that ensued he said, in fact, referring to his own original address :

> That speech was delivered under circumstances of the utmost publicity. According to my reading of it, it indicates a campaign, not secret at all, but perfectly open and above-board, for the defence of the progressive and self-help movement in Ireland against a party who are organised to crush it. The essence of this campaign is to bid Irishmen look for help to themselves and not to Westminster. To people whose eyes are unwaveringly fixed on Westminster as the only source of benefit to Ireland, every self-help movement in the latter country is naturally obnoxious. Their alarm, their anger, and the depths of misrepresentation and meanness to which they are ready to descend in order to keep the mind of the country riveted on Westminster and on themselves is a good measure of their consciousness that wholesomer and manlier ideals are spreading among the Irish people.

The whole business created a considerable stir at the time but probably, before the controversy had died down, it did Dillon and his friends more harm than it did either Plunkett, Rolleston, or the I.A.O.S. At any rate Rolleston was able to write in an article in *Land and Water* in October 1916, that the number of co-operative societies of all varieties in Ireland—for dairying, for agriculture, for rural credit, for poultry, and for other purposes—had increased to nearly one thousand and that their united trade was £3,000,000 per annum.

There was as a matter of fact a certain amount of excuse for Dillon's assumption that Rolleston was an official of the I.A.O.S., because he had always been closely associated with Plunkett and had given him all the help he could in connection with the launching and carrying on of his movement. When therefore in 1899 Ireland was given a Department of Agriculture and Technical Instruction separate from the Department at Whitehall and when Plunkett accepted the Vice-Presidency of it, he being at that time a Unionist Member

6

of Parliament, it is not surprising that he took Rolleston with him as 'Organiser of Lectures', a position he held until 1905.

In his new capacity T. W. R. gave himself very little rest and devoted his energies mainly to furthering the interests of the same home and rural industries with which, as Managing Director of the Irish Industries Association, he had already been so closely connected. He not only arranged and organised the whole lecture programme of an energetic Department on both Agricultural and Industrial subjects but himself travelled from end to end of the country encouraging and stimulating the grand work that was being done. This was work he loved ; he knew the Irish country people and peasant folk and they knew, admired, and trusted him.

He set high standards for the rural industries to work to and above all advocated one of his most cherished beliefs, namely that Ireland's future could be great and prosperous if the work done were truly Irish and if, in laying the foundations on which great industries could be built, she drew as heavily as possible on what was worth-while in Ireland's past.

In many, if not in all, of the Rural Industries which were at that time beginning to make their way, the question of design was of outstanding importance ; wood-carving, metal work, lace-making, carpet manufacture, and glass-making may be instanced in this connection and it will be of interest to read a report of one of Rolleston's lectures on the matter delivered at Letterkenny in December 1902. The subject was 'Artistic Industries', and it will be noted that the high standards set were the same as those he had urged on the Irish writers in another sphere of activity six years earlier. Rolleston, in fact, wanted the industry of the future to draw its inspiration from the beauty and romance of the past and to be Irish in every joint and fibre. I have not been able to find the full text of this particular lecture, the account which follows being taken from the *Derry Journal* of 19 December 1902 :

The Literary Institute at Letterkenny was crowded to the doors on Tuesday evening when Mr. T. W. Rolleston of the Department of Agriculture and Technical Instruction lectured there. The subject of the discourse was 'Artistic Industries' and the lecturer—able, cultured, and accomplished gentleman that he is—treated it in a manner highly instructive to all, and with a rare and charming flow of language, so simply descriptive in its every word that the splendid audience followed his address from beginning to end with close and earnest attention and with minds seemingly focussed on the thought ' What might we do and have not done '.

Verily the lecture was in the nature of a revelation. Mr. Rolleston did not twist the story beyond its meaning. He went back into the past, the great and wonderful past of Ireland's successes in artistic fields, the past where all was noble, worthy, edifying, and to be desired. Arguing from the glory of that past he showed in his own happy style that Ireland is not yet dead to the artistic sense of the beautiful in great things, but that with proper encouragement and fostering care she will excel in delicate art and again become worthy of the position she held in days gone by. Signs of that happy time are not indeed wanting, though so far we have nothing that is fit to be compared with much that was achieved of old in the field of artistic production.

Such lectures as that of Mr. Rolleston teach people a valuable lesson and bring prominently before them their failings and shortcomings in a very important direction ; they must undoubtedly stimulate them to a grand endeavour to make our country again as notable as it was in the golden past.

Mr. Rolleston, who was warmly greeted, began his lecture by pointing out the importance of the artistic industries in the economic life of a nation. The instinct for art was one of the deepest and oldest in humanity ; it was found in all stages of human development. From the Stone Age to the highest modern civilisation man had always endeavoured to add the elements of beauty and decoration to the things which he manufactured primarily for utilitarian purposes. Dealing with the question of what art really consisted of, the lecturer showed a slide of an ancient cromlech, and after that a beautiful illustration of a Greek Temple, and explained how the latter developed from the former under the influence of the artistic impulse. Art was really nothing but a vivid expression of life, and people delighted in it because they delighted in life itself. As applied to objects of use the effect of art was obtained when they were made to look as if they were doing the work for which they were intended. That gave an expression of vital energy to the form of the object ; that expression of energy was art.

After showing a number of illustrations to demonstrate this point, the lecturer dealt with the question of decoration. Art in the *decoration* was the same thing as art in the *form* of an object ; it gave life to it. People commonly spoke of a ' dead wall ', meaning thereby a blank, unchanging surface ; but introduce into that some glow of colour, some play of light and shade, some architectural features—such as arcades or niches—and you put life into your dead wall at once, for the law of life is eternal change. It was not, however, a disorderly, chaotic sort of change, but a change preceded by certain laws of order and rhythm. Mr. Rolleston exemplified this with some beautiful illustrations showing the difference between good and bad designing in the lace-making industry, to be found in so many parts of Donegal.

Incidentally Mr. Rolleston remarked that he had sometimes seen girls making the most beautiful laces and embroideries, but themselves having torn aprons and untidy hair and looking anything but artistic objects.

This was beginning at the wrong end. An art could not be permanently planted in a country on the same lines as an ordinary commercial industry. People must care for it for its own sake, and it must begin at home ; it must be made as familiar in the cottages and small towns as in great cities or it would not be a permanent and wholesome growth. Some slides illustrating peasant life and costume on the Continent were shown in connection with this point, particularly the interiors of two churches in Tyrol and in Bavaria, where the decorative work was done entirely by the hands of the villagers themselves.

Examples of the work done in Ireland by the Belgian wood-carvers of the ' Guild of St. Luke ' were then shown, and Mr. Rolleston asked how it came that foreign artists had to be called in to carve the figures of Irish saints in Irish churches. Among these was a figure of St. Connlaoch, the founder of the first technical art school in Christian Ireland. The beautiful stone work done by the O'Sheas in the engineering school of Trinity College, in the Oxford University Museum, and elsewhere was then shown as an example of what Irish hands and brains, when properly trained, could accomplish.

Irish workmanship, Mr. Rolleston said, should be trained till it was fit to compete with any other, but he had no sympathy at all with the practice of obtaining bad Irish work rather than good foreign work. It was not only lowering the standard and spoiling our future chances of real success, but often resulted in putting up works which would exercise a bad influence on the taste of those who habitually saw them.

Mr. Rolleston concluded his lecture by exhibiting a series of very beautiful slides showing examples of the finest Irish work, both from pagan and Christian times, and ending with an illustration of the famous Ardagh Chalice, even the base of which was covered with rich and exquisite ornamentation arranged on concentric circles around a large crystal. The artist who thus adorned the Ardagh Chalice worked in the same spirit as the Belgian wood-carver who was lately decorating Kilkenny Cathedral. A visitor who looked in while the work was going on observed him finishing a piece of carving with great care, though it was in a dark angle of the church ; he asked, ' Why do you spend so much time and trouble over that, when no one will ever see it ? ' The man looked up and answered simply, ' God sees it '. That was the true spirit of the artist. It would have been all the same whether he were doing a piece of work in a sacred edifice or whether it were a writing-table or a wooden spoon ; whatever the true artist makes he makes with love and care, for he works for his ideal and not for the eye of man. That was the spirit we must see in Ireland if art was to flourish there as it once did—when a glorious object like the Cross of Cong could be made in the town of Roscommon. Their spirit of originality had been stifled by the slavish spirit of imitation of foreign ways and things which had prevailed so long. They were now, however, finding their way back to the true sources of Irish intellectual and spiritual life, and re-uniting the country with its past. On these lines they might hope eventually to restore to Ireland an artistic culture which would enable them to produce works of beauty not inferior to those relics of the past on which Celtic genius had set its immortal seal.

The Ardagh Chalice and the Cross of Cong are probably the two most beautiful things the hands of men have ever made. Of the former it has been aptly said that it appears to be the work of angels rather than of men. The Cross of Cong was made in the year 1123 by order of King Furlough O'Conor as a shrine for a portion of the True Cross which had been given to the Irish King by the Pope. Its maker was Maeljean Mac Brathdan O'Echan. Both the Chalice and the Cross are in the National Museum in Dublin and are worth journeying across the world to see.

In 1904 these two priceless objects formed part of the Irish Historic Loan Collection which was sent to the great Exhibition at St. Louis. T. W. Rolleston went in charge of that collection, a very heavy responsibility, as most of the examples of ancient Irish art which were entrusted to his care were—and are— of course quite irreplaceable. St. Patrick's Bell, for example, has an unbroken history which extends back to the fifth century.

Rolleston came back from that visit to the United States very much impressed with what he had seen and heard and learnt in that country. On the whole his impression was favourable, but he did not miss the evils that have been allowed to grow and flourish in America. He lectured on his visit at Wexford not long after his return and it might be interesting to compare this very vivid picture of American business, politics, and administration in 1904 with their condition to-day, thirty-five years later. He said, amongst other things :

In Europe, though all men are tolerably equal before the law, there are, from the highest class to the lowest, multitudes of invisible barriers which keep men from passing readily from one class of society to another. A man of genius, a man of dauntless energy and perseverance can get through them ; but in America these barriers hardly exist at all. Anybody may be anything. Personal qualities tell with direct and irresistible effect. All men are not equal in America, but the tendency of the system is to give them all an equality of opportunity. Nor does America ever forget that all men—or not quite that ; I must limit the statement by saying ' all white men '—are equal in respect of their common humanity . . . Theodore Roosevelt, the large-hearted and large-brained man who sits on the Presidential throne at present, is a man of old family, of much inherited wealth, and University breeding. The greatest President before him, Abraham Lincoln, began life as a woodchopper. Roosevelt's origin counted neither for nor against him ; Lincoln's counted neither for nor against *him*.   America recognised the man in both of them ; and America loves a man.

After touching on the subject of free education and the splendid equipment and fittings in American schools, Rolleston went on :

There are, however, some very dark features in American life, and I cannot leave the subject without referring to some of them.   The tremendous business energy of America has led to the formation of vast industrial financial trusts and syndicates and these have gathered to themselves an amount of power which they use with an unscrupulousness undreamt of over here.   They secure themselves against competition from without by a tariff system of the greatest stringency, and from within by ruthlessly crushing out, often by criminal means, all competitors whom they cannot absorb.   The big men who manage the industrial and financial life of the U.S.A. do not go into politics themselves, but they run the men who do.   The interests at stake are so great that they find it pays them to spend vast sums in getting control of the Legislatures, of the Judiciary, and, worst of all, the police ; with the result that all these institutions are deeply tainted with corruption.   They are aided in this by the fact that Judgeships in America are ridiculously underpaid and that Civil Servants are removable.   The statistics of crime in the United States bear witness to this state of things—inefficiency naturally arising from corruption in the civil administration.   Thus, in the case of one class of crime—that of homicide of all kinds, murder, and manslaughter—we find that the number per year has risen in the States out of all proportion to the growth of population.   In 1885 there were 1,803 homicides in the States—or 32 per million of the population.   In 1904 there were 8,482, or over 104 per million of the population.   The number of executions which resulted was only one for every 73 crimes.   Homicides in the United Kingdom are about 500 per annum, or $12\frac{1}{2}$ per million of the population.   These figures are a terrible warning against the evils that come from running the great public services of the State in the interests of political parties, which themselves are largely run in the interests of huge financial trusts and syndicates.

But for all the gloominess of this picture Rolleston saw great things ahead for the United States of America, and he concluded by saying :

I believe those of you who are young will see the day when the transforming and vitalising power of American ideas will reach across the Atlantic and touch to new life and growth the vast populations of Europe who toil in the twilight of their ignorance, under the oppression of ancient despotisms which, now mostly dead as laws, survive with almost equal tyranny as traditions and customs.

That prophecy can hardly be said to have come true as yet. Rolleston's visit to America, which extended over four months, was perhaps the most interesting of his experiences during the five years he spent with the Department of Agriculture. But he was happiest there when his work took him away from the office in Upper Merrion Street and into the country on one of his many lecturing and inspection tours. To tell the truth, Rolleston did not like offices or routine ; his spirit was much too free and was too intolerant of the formality and system that are inseparable from office work ever to have been long content in such surroundings. He was very sensitive to atmosphere and felt, which was probably quite true, that he could work best in his own setting, in his own study, sitting in his own chair—always the same one made of carved oak—with the pictures he loved on the walls, and the wife and family he loved too to come and drag him away when it was absolutely necessary that he should realise that one must eat to live. Left to himself he would never have been in time for a meal ; there was always something he wanted to finish first, and many a time have I seen Maud, my stepmother, literally take the pen out of his hand and put it down before she led him, gently and humorously protesting, into the dining-room.

Once there, however, his work would be forgotten ; he had the priceless faculty of being able to clear his mind at any moment of the things that may have been bothering it and to change from the painstaking student and writer and thinker into a gay and delightful husband and father. Under such conditions he was happy, and one must be happy and contented in order to be able to do good work. The conditions that suited him could not be created in an office.

I do not think therefore that my father's personal regret was very deep when in 1905 Plunkett was succeeded at the Department by T. W. Russell and Rolleston necessarily left the service of the Government at the same time. He would probably not have joined it at all in the first place had it not been for his desire to help Plunkett to get the Department going.

Plunkett's departure was brought about by the fact that it had been decided that the Vice-President of the Department of Agriculture should have a seat in Parliament and Plunkett had been defeated for South Dublin in 1900. A seat was offered to him but its acceptance would have necessitated his changing his political colours ; this he would not do. Another man was therefore found who was politically satisfactory and so T. W. Russell stepped into Plunkett's shoes. Despite the identity of their initials T. W. Rolleston and T. W. Russell could not possibly have worked together.

This event really terminated by father's active work for the industrial regeneration of Ireland ; thereafter he devoted his energies to forwarding the activities of the Gaelic League and to his own writings, which are dealt with elsewhere in this volume.

An attempt was made, however, two years later to draw him back into official life, but, although the invitation to do so came almost in the form of a Royal Command, he declined it.

It will be remembered that in 1907 a sensation was caused by the announcement that the Irish Crown Jewels had been stolen from Dublin Castle. These priceless heirlooms had been in the care and custody of the Ulster King of Arms—the head of the College of Heralds in Ireland—a position held at that time by Sir Arthur Vicars. It was alleged that this astounding theft had been made possible by laxity in the department presided over by Vicars and his resignation was requested. Vicars, however, thought that such action on his part, following immediately on the theft itself, would be tantamount to an admission that he was in some way to blame. In fact, in view of the extraordinary rumours and ridiculous stories that were circulated, it is quite possible—certain indeed—that Vicars' voluntary resignation would have been regarded as an admission that he had stolen the jewels himself or had at least been a party to the theft.

However that may be my father was both surprised and gratified to receive the following letter from Lord Aberdeen, who was then Lord Lieutenant of Ireland :

VICEREGAL LODGE,
DUBLIN
DEC. 17, '07

PRIVATE

DEAR MR. ROLLESTON,

With the direct and definite approval of the King, I write to offer for your acceptance the post of Ulster King of Arms, which, in connection with the complete reconstitution of the Staff of that Office, will immediately become vacant.

I sincerely hope that it will be agreeable to you to take the position. The salary is £500 per annum.

I regret that no retiring pension is attached, but on the other hand the age limit is, in this case, 70.

I shall be glad to offer any further information and I would also be very pleased to see you here.

I remain

Very truly yours,

ABERDEEN.

It was a tempting offer but there were various considerations which induced him to decline the post and the Knighthood that always went with it.

Whether Vicars did ultimately resign or whether his office was declared vacant I am not now certain, but I do know that my father was afterwards very glad for another reason that he had refused to take his place. Vicars and he were personal friends, and at the time Lord Aberdeen wrote the above letter, Vicars was still the holder of the post. I remember my father saying that he would have been very upset if it had appeared that he had accepted the appointment while his friend was still holding it and refusing to resign ; he thought of course that Vicars *had* resigned and did not know the true position till later. There were doubtless many who would have said that he had been, at the best, too ready to accept a lucrative post before it had actually been vacated ; and others would have accused him of taking advantage of Vicars' misfortune to benefit himself.

But I think an important consideration in his mind was the fact that an alliance in an official capacity with Dublin Castle might have hampered any work he might still be able to do for Ireland and would have prejudiced any influence he could have exerted in Irish public life. The holder of the office of Lord-Lieutenant, the representative of the King or Queen of England and, apparently, of the English Government—the figurehead of the ship of state when it navigated Irish waters—could not hope to be liked in a country where it was considered patriotic to profess hatred of England and everything English. Round the Lord-Lieutenant at Dublin Castle and the Vice-

regal Lodge there revolved the minions of the foreign law—
' Castle Officials '—and from or through them came the laws
and regulations which provided the machinery of administration. These were all regarded as interlopers, foreigners, and
objects of suspicion. The degree with which they were dis-
liked varied of course with the individual, but to be a Castle
Official, even in such a post as Ulster King of Arms, would
have handicapped men like Plunkett, Rolleston, George Russell,
and those others whose every effort was always directed
towards smoothing out the differences between Nationalist
and Unionist, Protestant and Roman Catholic, landlord and
tenant, gentry and peasantry, by giving them all a common
industrial interest in the welfare of their country.

There was another difference too which maintained a wide
breach between the Castle people and the general population.
From the Lord-Lieutenant downwards the officials all enjoyed
good salaries ; they were wealthy, or at least well off, by
comparison with the peasantry, who were in distress if an acre
of potatoes were to be lost. Some Lord-Lieutenants rather
accentuated this difference by keeping up a style and by entertaining in a manner the lavishness of which was, to say the least
of it, in rather bad taste when displayed before the eyes of a
desperately poor people. Lady Fingall in her book of reminiscences relates that when Lord Dudley came to Ireland as
Viceroy in 1902 ' he was the spoilt child of fortune. His father
had been the richest man in England.' In spite, Lady Fingall
goes on, of Lord Dudley's remaining ' amazingly unspoilt ',
she writes of the ' brilliance and extravagance of the Dudley
Season. In their first year in Ireland the Dudleys had spent
£80,000. Their salary was £20,000.' Then again : ' There
were thirty-two black horses hired from Dolland of London.
About four of them were used regularly, but the rest were used
only twice a year—at the Horse Show and Punchestown.
But all the thirty-two were kept exercised and paid for all the
year round.'

Lady Fingall does not comment on this display of wealth ;
in fact she gives the impression of thinking it rather amusing
than otherwise ; but it made no appeal to the Irish people
and was in truth in rather bad taste.

The Aberdeens must be acquitted of erring in the same
direction ; but, for all that, they were not any more successful

or any less so, than other holders of the difficult positions of
Viceroy and Vicereine of Ireland, and when later on Lord
Aberdeen was elevated to a Marquisate and proposed to take
the additional title of ' Tara ' the outcry in Ireland was almost
ferocious. Lord Aberdeen had only intended this as a compliment, but the Irish were not prepared to tolerate the appro-
priation by a Scot of the name of the most sacred spot in all
Ireland ; so the new Marquis fell back on the dative form of
the same name—' Temair '.

Rolleston left the Department of Agriculture in 1905 and,
there being nothing further to keep him actually in Dublin,
he thought he would try the life of a country gentleman ;
he decided at the same time to take the opportunity of writing
the book on philosophical subjects which had been taking shape
in his brain for many years.[1] He shaved his beard, survived
an attack of double pneumonia, and moved to the country,
to Hollywood House, near the village of Glenealy, in County
Wicklow. But the experiment was not an unqualified success;
though my father was glad of the peace and quiet of the
country in which to write ' Parallel Paths ', yet he did rather
miss his many friends in Dublin, and sometimes found himself
a little hampered in putting together his weekly letter for one
of the London papers because of his absence from the centre
of Irish affairs. He had always loved the country, especially
the soft beauty of County Wicklow, and the massive old beech
trees in the grounds of Hollywood were a source of never-
ending admiration to him ; but, when *The Times* in 1909
invited him to take charge of the German section of *The
Times Literary Supplement*, the manifest advantages of accepting outweighed other considerations and he moved his home
to Hampstead.

This phase of Rolleston's life, which might properly be
called the industrial phase, would not be complete without
referring to at least one other proposal whereby he thought
Ireland could be benefited. Hitherto I have touched only on
activities of what might be called the ' self-help ' kind, that is
to say those methods by which Ireland, by her own internal
efforts, might seek to increase her prosperity. But it was not
unreasonable, Rolleston thought, that England should be
asked to assist. There was, therefore, a proposal, about which

[1] See p. 159.

I cannot now find anything in writing, that the Government should offer financial inducements to English manufacturers who, desiring to extend their businesses by erecting additional factories, would place those factories in Ireland. Money for such enterprises, my father suggested, could be lent by the Government at a nominal rate of interest or the manufacturers could be guaranteed against any loss of profits that might result from extra freight and handling charges between Irish ports and the English market.

If such a plan had been put into at all general operation it would have given work to thousands of Irishmen and women in other than purely agricultural and seasonal pursuits and would have led to the more extended use of Irish ports and harbours, both for the landing of raw materials from abroad and the shipment of finished products. This development of harbours would also have given employment in the construction of wharves and jetties, in building store-houses and transit sheds, in making additional railways and railway sidings, and in a host of indirect ways.

It can hardly be doubted that such a scheme would have been of enormous benefit to the country and would, in addition to levelling up the financial positions of Ulster and the South, have also stimulated the home and cottage industries by increasing the average purchasing power of the Irish people. It would also have helped materially to eliminate the long periods of idleness to which a purely agricultural population is necessarily condemned. If the hoped-for results had been achieved the greater contentment of the people and the distraction of their thoughts from their country's grievances would have been acquisitions on the credit side of the Anglo-Irish ledger which would have been cheap at almost any price.

Nothing, however, came of the idea nor of a more concrete and equally promising scheme whereby Galway or some other suitable Western Harbour was to be developed as a trans-Atlantic shipping port in conjunction with a new cross-country railway and a train-ferry or tunnel to cover the short sea-route between Ireland and Scotland. The idea received a good deal of publicity, the credit for it being generally given to George Moore. Actually, however, the scheme was Rolleston's, as Moore acknowledged when in 1920 he dedicated a reprint of *Esther Waters* to my father.   Here is what he called his ' Epistle Dedicatory ' :

MY DEAR ROLLESTON,

It is quite in accordance with the humour of the great Aristophanes above us, beneath us, within us, without us, that an Irishman should write a book as characteristically English as ' Don Quixote ' is Spanish, and when the author of *Esther Waters* dedicates his work to another Irishman it must be plain to all that he is holding the mirror up to nature.   But there is another reason why I should dedicate this book to you.   You are an Irish Protestant like myself, and you could always love Ireland without hating England and . . . But I am past my patience trying to find logic in a dedication which is an outburst of friendly feeling for an old friend.

It would be pleasant to look down the last five-and-twenty years, but I will look no further than yesteryear, when we were engaged in trying to wheedle the English public into accepting the only solution (yours) of the Irish difficulty— a line of railway linking a western harbour with a northern tunnel joining Ireland to Scotland.   We failed, of course, in practical result (the official mind repels reason), but our adventure was not without moral gain, for two Irishmen did set out ' to strike a blow for Ireland ' without coming to blows. How shall we explain it : that the great Aristophanes above us, beneath us, within us, without us, willed it so ? and that his divine humour was not content with less than that the letters that you wrote and that I signed must be better written than those you signed yourself.

> It is a modest creed, and yet
> Pleasant if one considers it . . .

to think that your solicitude for others compelled you to give your best to your friend.

Yours always,

GEORGE MOORE.

It was not always easy to get publicity for this scheme in England and I remember one occasion when both my father and Moore were very angry because, in an article on Irish affairs signed by Moore but written by Rolleston for the

Manchester Guardian, that paper omitted the portion which advocated this proposal as a means of helping to settle the Irish question. The interests of Manchester with its £20,000,000 Ship-Canal and of Liverpool would of course have been adversely affected by a commercial harbour on anything like a large scale at Galway. The answer of Irishmen to this and all such objections is that Ireland was supposed to be part of a *United* Kingdom in which it was fair to assume that favours and opportunities should be more or less evenly distributed.

One might, however, write books on the subject of the use that could be made of Ireland in the interests of the Empire, as well as of the dangers that can come from an Ireland outside the Empire. As far as that country herself is concerned they would all boil down to one objective—the same one at which Rolleston aimed and the one which, in spite of all that has passed in the interval, is still capable of providing a solution of the Irish question : that is, to make the commercial and industrial conditions of the South comparable to those of the North. When that has been done there will no longer be an Irish problem ; but Ireland cannot do it with only her own resources on which to rely.

Since the above was written the International crisis of September 1938 has passed into history, leaving, among other legacies, a vivid realisation by the people of Great Britain of their vulnerability to attack from the air. As far as the individual citizen is concerned everything possible is probably being done by the provision of gas masks, shelters, and so on, and also by arranging for the evacuation of children from crowded cities that might become death-traps ; camps are to be provided in the country where schools can be re-established away from the proximity of legitimate objectives for enemy bombs.

But besides caring for the individual there are other even more vital considerations. Our naval bases, shipping ports, and industries are all within what might prove to be fatally easy reach of aircraft operating from the continent of Europe, and it would be difficult to imagine a more promising hunting-ground for hostile submarines operating against our vital sea communications than is provided by the narrow approaches to our western and southern coasts and the Thames estuary.

These conditions present an ideal basis on which to negotiate a new agreement between England and Southern Ireland, an agreement which would, moreover, be of incalculable value to both countries, and indeed to the whole British Empire.

The best preliminary defence against air attack is to establish oneself as far away as possible from the aircraft bases from which the attack may come, and the west of Ireland is as far as one can get in the British Isles. It is there in Galway Bay or Clew Bay or elsewhere that naval bases and trans-ocean shipping ports should have been constructed years ago. It is in Ireland, where hydro-electric power could perhaps make up for the lack of coal, that many war-time industries should have been established. It is in Ireland that the schools and children's camps should now be built ; the *Queen Mary* and *Queen Elizabeth*, whose value in war-time is highly problematical on account of their great size, could ship the children across in a very short time. It is at Irish ports and in Irish harbours that merchant craft from overseas should unload their precious cargoes of food and raw materials in time of war, thus enormously simplifying the problem of trade protection. The Irish Sea, the English Channel, the Bristol Channel, and the northern approaches to Glasgow and Liverpool are so narrow and restricted in area that enemy submarines might have little difficulty in patrolling them all and taking a perhaps disastrous toll of our essential supplies and of the vessels that must carry them. The same vessels, however, making for any port in the north, west, or south of Ireland will have the whole open ocean in which to elude a waiting submarine ; there is an almost infinite variety of directions from which ships can approach Irish destinations and the chances of their getting through successfully are increased proportionately.

In just about the same proportion will the difficulties of the submarines be increased ; the number required to keep effective watch on the approaches to Galway Bay would be at least ten times the number that could paralyse shipping in the vicinity of the Severn estuary or the Clyde. Further to that, each submarine watching the approaches to the west of Ireland would have many hundreds of miles added to her voyage out and home and would therefore find the time she could spend on her station seriously reduced. Nor would such submarines be able, in bad weather, to find convenient places off the Irish coast where the water would be shallow enough to enable them to lie on the bottom till the gale had blown itself out. Submarines can do this almost anywhere east of a line from Cape Ushant to Queenstown ; forcing them to operate further west will be enlisting the elements on our side in a very practical way.

It would be labouring the obvious to elaborate any further on the extreme value of Ireland from this point of view, though it may be stated that the same arguments hold good where air attack is concerned. A hostile aeroplane could be over London within seven minutes, or Birmingham within twenty minutes, of crossing our east coast. This gives no time to speak of in which to put last-minute defence preparations into motion, to get people under cover, to man guns, or do anything else necessary to beat off or meet the attack.

An additional precious hour could be added to these intervals if the enemy had to reach an objective in the west of Ireland, say in the neighbourhood of Limerick or Roscommon ; and the defence would have greatly increased opportunities of bringing the raiders down before their objective had been reached at all. The enemy too would have to carry more petrol and therefore fewer bombs on the longer flight. Again the point need not be laboured.

The obstacle to making use of Ireland in this way, to which geography so clearly points, is of course the attitude of Mr. de Valera's government ; an essential first step would have to be the re-incorporation of Ireland in the United Kingdom, the advantages of which to both countries are so manifest that it should not be impossible for men of goodwill on both sides of the Irish Sea to bring about that very desirable end.

Mr. de Valera has said that he does not mind Ireland being poor provided she is free. Poor she certainly is, but freedom is still for her a very far thing. As recently as the early part of 1939 Mr. de Valera pointed out that, if his country is to continue to supply England with food in time of war, she cannot hope to remain neutral. But surely no conception of 'freedom' would place it beyond the power of the 'free' country to say whether or not she will remain neutral or make war ? Freedom in this respect is therefore an entire myth where Southern Ireland is concerned.

As far as individual liberty is affected I do not think that even Mr. de Valera, if he were to consider the position of other nationals, would maintain that there is on this earth to-day a nation whose citizens are less restricted as to what they may say or do than the British people. Within the widest limits we may act and write pretty much what we like and our political liberty amazes other peoples who are less fortunately placed. It was an Irishman, Mr. James M. Dillon, Deputy Leader of the Irish Opposition, whom I heard about two years ago give the best possible definition of our political liberty when he said it was such that a man could criticise the Government— and ' live to do it again '. I do not say that citizens of Mr. de Valera's Republic are any less free as individuals, but I do maintain that in this respect they will be surrendering nothing by again becoming citizens of a United Kingdom.

Again, in spite of Ireland's efforts to find other markets for her exports, she still sells ninety per cent of her produce to England. This means in plain language that England could, with a stroke of the pen, reduce Ireland to a state of penury ; such action too would certainly find favour in the Dominions and Colonies and in the Argentine from whom purchases could then be greatly increased. Can a country be called free when she is so irrevocably shackled to another and is financially at that other nation's mercy ?

As an integral part of the United Kingdom, becoming such by a re-enactment in substance of the Act of Union of 1801, Ireland's status in war-time will be altered not one iota but her position as an exporter will be placed beyond peril. Ireland has in fact everything to gain—including the respect of the rest of the world—and nothing whatever to lose by agreeing to this very sensible step. The country badly needs capital for development, for the reorganisation of her railways, for the construction of oversea ports, and for a myriad other purposes ; this England must provide as her part of the bargain. New railways too will be needed to link the new western ports with the east coast, and the construction of a tunnel, if prac-ticable, between Ireland and Scotland so strongly advocated by my father and others should be put in hand. If this were not possible from an engineering point of view a train-ferry

7

from Larne or Belfast Lough will serve the purpose. In war-time it should be quite possible to give it efficient protection by means of minefields to north and south and by other means such as were used during the Great War to guard the Straits of Dover.

Ulster can have no possible objection to such an agreement and, as far as the re-uniting of Ireland is concerned—a matter very near to Mr. de Valera's heart—will this not have been achieved when Southern Ireland has returned to the Union? The consequent identity of interests between the two parts of the country will obliterate the boundary and the disappearance of the customs posts will soon remove all evidence that there ever was a boundary at all.

III

PSYCHIC AND RECREATIONAL

HITHERTO I have dealt with the two main interests that absorbed my father's attention—Anglo-Irish Literature and the solution of his country's difficulties ; I propose now to touch on some subsidiary interests, some of them providing matter for serious study and others being merely hobbies and recreations.

T. W. Rolleston was intensely interested in things psychic, as indeed who, born and brought up in Ireland, could fail to be. His approach to the supernatural, however, was not in the usual Irish way, through fear or respect or just a blind belief that ' these things are so ' and that's all there is about it. As with every other matter which came within the wide range of his intellectual view he ' wanted to know '. Given more leisure and a less practical mind he would probably have thrown himself whole-heartedly into the business of investigating the mysterious. He was a member of the Society for Psychical Research and an acquaintance of Sir Oliver Lodge.

But Rolleston was not by any means a fanatic on the subject and most emphatically he was not a spiritualist. He knew there was ' something ' we didn't understand and he wanted to find out what it was. His efforts in this direction were aimed towards an endeavour to explain the supernatural in terms of the natural—natural to ordinary mortals that is. He was almost excited when Sir William F. Barrett, F.R.S., sent him a copy of his *On the Threshold of the Unseen* because in part the author seemed to account for extraordinary happenings such as tables, chairs, and so forth rising from the floor apparently unaided, in physical terms. I remember his giving us an account of a séance he had attended one afternoon at, I think, Sir Oliver Lodge's house, when articles like rulers, inkstands, books, &c., had risen from the table and floated without visible human aid through one window and back through the other to come to rest again on the table.

These things didn't frighten Rolleston as they might some people, and no one who knew him could doubt for a moment that, if he said he saw them, then see them he did ; he was quite incapable of inventing on this, or any other, subject. He dismissed trickery in cases where the other people concerned were obviously above suspicion and could have had no possible motive to serve ; but he *did* want to find out the cause of the strange things he saw. He failed to do so of course any more satisfactorily than any one else.

Most Irish people accept the supernatural as part and parcel of their everyday lives but they are careful—very careful—not to do anything which might offend or annoy the Sidhe,[1] the Fairies, the ' Little People '. They have their recognised preserves and nothing would induce an Irish man or woman to trespass thereon. When Stopford Brooke was staying with my father and stepmother in Donegal he expressed the Irish reverence and respect—' fear ' is not quite the right word— for the Little People in this entry in his diary :

The wild moor was pleasant, and the sun shone on the grey rocks and heather and the dark ditches cut deep into the bog-land. The river ran below among its trees and far away, beyond the jaws of the Bay, the Sligo mountains rose flat-topped and blue over the blue waters. Few were the sounds, for few are the cattle that graze on hills where no pleasant grass abides. The greenest spots are the tumuli, of which there are many here, that cover the burial places of ancient heroes and chiefs. But the peasantry will not allow their cattle even to walk over these green mounds. That would offend the Fairy Folk who dwell in them, and some misfortune would befall the cattle or their owners. One lives in Ireland in the constant presence of the fairy world. They touch life at every point—as fully believed in as the Virgin and the Saints. No matter from what scientific world one comes, the fairy faith grows into one's imagination in the West of Ireland. I seemed to see the gods of the sea swimming far below in the blue depths as I looked down from the cliffs, and I went out of the Inn in the moonlight to see the Shee come riding out of the grassy mounds—nor was it difficult to see them.

This belief in the Sidhe is accounted for in Rolleston's *Myths and Legends of the Celtic Race*, the explanation being not his own but that which has been handed down in Ireland for innumerable centuries. After telling how Ireland was at one time peopled by the Danaans, or people of the Goddess Dana,

[1] Pronounced ' Shee '.

till the Milesians came to seize the island from them, the story continues :

A great battle with the Danaans at Telltown then follows. The three Kings and three Queens of the Danaans, with many of their people, are slain, and the children of Miled—the last of the mythical invaders of Ireland—enter upon the sovranty of Ireland. But the people of Dana do not withdraw. By their magic art they cast over themselves a veil of invisibility, which they can put on and off as they choose. There are two Irelands henceforward, the spiritual and the earthly. The Danaans dwell in the spiritual Ireland, which is portioned out among them by their great overlord, the Dagda. Where the human eye can see but green mounds and ramparts, the relics of ruined fortresses or sepulchres, there rise the fairy palaces of the defeated divinities ; there they hold their revels in eternal sunshine, nourished by the magic meat and ale that give them undying youth and beauty ; and thence they come forth at times to mingle with mortal men in love or in war. The ancient mythical literature conceives them as heroic and splendid in strength and beauty. In later times, and as Christian influences grew stronger, they dwindle into fairies, the People of the Sidhe ; but they have never wholly perished ; to this day the Land of Youth and its inhabitants live in the imagination of the Irish peasant.

The old mythological deities of the Irish have not therefore ceased to exist, as those of other mythologies have done. They are still there, co-existing in their subterranean palaces and feasting places with the human race living above-ground. This may in part explain the Irish failure to appreciate the passage of time. While the figures of Greek mythology, for example, are admitted now to be dead and therefore without further influence, those of Ireland exist to this very day, and their period lives with them—for it is eternal. Yesterday is still here in Ireland and always has been. Even Eriu, wife of MacGrené, one of the three Danaan Kings, still lives, as Rolleston points out, in the poetic name for Ireland, which is the dative form of Eriu—Erinn.

To say that Ireland teems with ' ghosts ' and supernatural manifestations of all kinds is hardly overstating the case. One is compelled to believe in them whether one likes it or not, as witness the occasion when a whole school—masters, boys, and every one—turned out on three successive nights to try to locate a banshee. The school was St. Columba's College and the episode took place in about 1897. I was not there myself at the time but both my elder brothers were. A boy called Pratt was taken ill and moved to the school

Infirmary. Getting worse his father was summoned and a few days after his arrival the whole school was awakened during the night by the wailing of a banshee in the direction of the wood which fringed the school grounds. Every one turned out and the wood, and indeed the whole vicinity, were scoured from end to end, but of course with no success. Next night the same thing happened again with the same result and the boy's father said that if the banshee were heard again his boy would not live. The banshee came again on the third night and before the morning young Pratt had died.

This is only one perfectly authenticated record of the ' appearance ' of this particular portent of death, a kind of heirloom in certain Irish families. There is also the famous Leap Castle ghost, a horrible, half-human, half-animal creature which, covered with dirty looking brown hair, walks more or less upright and is the only known ghost which smells. Its coming is always heralded and accompanied by an appalling sickly stench. This dreadful apparition used to be seen most frequently by the children at Leap but has also appeared in the presence of grown-up people whose assurances must be accepted.

But perhaps the most extraordinary ghost story of all, and one which I do not think has ever before been published, was the experience of that Lord Dufferin who was afterwards one of India's most famous and successful Viceroys.[1] Lord Dufferin himself told the tale to my father, whom I have heard re-tell it many times.

When he was a young man Lord Dufferin was invited to visit a friend's house in Ireland ; there was a house-party to last a fortnight or so. In those days the coach was still the most usual method of making long journeys and when Lord Dufferin arrived in due course about half an hour before dinner he was met in the hall by his host, who mentioned in conversation that the party was now complete, Lord Dufferin being the last to arrive.

' But I daresay you would like to go straight to your room ', he continued, ' and have a clean-up. I'll introduce you to the others when we meet in the drawing-room before going in to dinner. Every one is dressing at the moment.'

[1] Since writing the above I have seen this story in a slightly different and shorter form in Harold Nicholson's *Helen's Tower*.

Lord Dufferin's room was in the front of the house and its main window, before which stood the dressing-table and mirror, was immediately over the front porch. This projected in the usual manner over the front steps, its flat roof being just below the level of Lord Dufferin's window.

While Lord Dufferin was standing in front of the dressing-table adjusting his tie or doing some other last-minute job before going downstairs he was surprised to hear a coach, identifiable as a coach-and-four by the clatter of hoofs and sound of wheels, coming up the avenue. An unexpected arrival was an event in the more remote parts of the country in those days and Lord Dufferin remembered that he had been told the house-party was complete. No other arrival was therefore expected and a natural curiosity impelled Lord Dufferin to pull the window curtain aside to see who got out of the coach, which by this time had pulled up at the front door.

The porch, however, prevented him from seeing more than the roof of the coach, the box-seat, and the backs of the horses ; these were illuminated by the light which streamed out through the front door, which had been opened to admit the new arrival. The only person Lord Dufferin could see, however, was the driver, who happened to have half turned round on his seat at the moment when Lord Dufferin looked out and was looking straight at him through his window and its drawn-back curtain. Lord Dufferin dropped the curtain, but not before he had noticed that the man on the box-seat was the most hideously repulsive creature he had ever seen. His face was almost diabolical in its ugliness and was unforgettably horrible. Lord Dufferin nearly shuddered as he wondered who could have such a dreadful looking coachman in his employ.

The coach drove away again and a minute or two later Lord Dufferin went down to the drawing-room. When introductions were over he found himself with his host and, more to make conversation perhaps than for any other reason, he asked who the new arrival might be.

' I thought you told me I was the last to arrive,' he said, ' and that I made the party complete.'

' But no one else has arrived,' replied his host.

' Well, I certainly saw a coach out of my window ; you'll

probably know whose it was because the driver was the most repulsive looking creature I've ever seen.' Lord Dufferin gave a brief description of the man, remarking that surely his host would know who it was who could be eccentric enough to employ such a curious type of servant.

' Oh,' said his host ; ' I was beginning to suspect what had happened. The coach is not real ; nor is the driver. It comes sometimes but doesn't mean anything unless the driver happens to look at some one. If he does that, the person he has looked at has invariably been killed in an accident or at any rate has died shortly afterwards. I hope he didn't look at you.'

Not wishing to upset the party Lord Dufferin did not say that the ghostly driver had in fact looked at him and the subject was not referred to again.

The house-party came to an end in due course and the guests went their various ways. Some time later Lord Dufferin found himself in Paris where he stayed at a hotel and occupied a room on one of the upper floors. Those were the early days of lifts and this hotel had one of the new appliances, which were not yet by any means accident-proof.

One morning, wishing to go down to breakfast, Lord Dufferin decided to try the lift. He walked to the end of his bedroom corridor and found that the cage was at a higher floor ; he summoned it and when it stopped at his level the door was opened ; he had one foot inside when he happened to glance at the man who was operating it. He was astonished to find himself face to face with the driver of the coach ; the face was quite unmistakable.

With considerable presence of mind he stepped back, murmuring something about there being a lot of people in the lift and not wanting to crowd them. Then he went down by the stairs. The lift continued its journey, but the rope broke, it crashed to the bottom, and all the occupants were killed.

But that is not the whole story. When the sensation and disturbance had died down—next morning perhaps—Lord Dufferin decided to find out something about the strange creature whom he had twice seen in such unusual circumstances. He went to the hotel manager and asked who the man was, suggesting, as an excuse for his curiosity, that he might perhaps contribute to any fund that might be opened for his widow or family.

'Well', said the manager, 'I'm afraid we cannot tell you anything because we don't know ourselves. He was not our regular liftman, who is sick. This man came before we had found a relief; he said he could drive a lift so, as people were waiting to use it, we put him straight to work without even asking his name. Nor have we or the police been able to find out anything since.'

One cannot help speculating on these things, but who is to explain them? T. W. Rolleston would have liked to be able to do so and, had he been able to devote more time and attention to this subject, which interested him intensely—though in an essentially sane manner—I have no doubt that his unique and tireless brain would have arrived at some sort of explanation. He did in fact in 1909 publish in, of all places, the *Irish Church Quarterly*, an intensely interesting article in which he summarised some of the conclusions he had reached in connection with ' supernatural ' matters. This article, called ' Some Recent Results of Psychical Research ', ends with a paragraph which demonstrates very well the essentially sane and logical manner in which my father approached this subject—and indeed all subjects which interested him :

The reader who is not acquainted with the records and other publications referred to in this article must understand that of the interesting and debatable matter contained in them only the barest fringe has here been touched. I think I am right in saying that hitherto little attention has been given in Ireland to this subject. I should wish to see the study of it promoted among us ; but a word of warning may be in place. It is not a subject to play with ; not a study to go into for the sake of mere childish curiosity and excitement. There may be grave dangers in it for ill-balanced minds. Sir William Crookes has somewhere declared that the spectacle of young people taking up table-rapping or planchette as a drawing-room diversion, an alternative to bridge or parlour games, makes him feel as if he saw a child going with a lighted match into a powder-magazine. Such a warning, from such a source, is not to be lightly disregarded. It could easily be reinforced by specific instances of the danger to morals and health which have resulted from the pursuit of occult investigations by the wrong people or in the wrong spirit. On the other hand, no one can study the lives and characters of men like Myers, Hodgson, and Henry Sidgwick, and at the same time suppose that there can be anything essentially evil and pernicious in the studies to which they devoted such great powers and on which they built such high hopes. Whether these hopes are ever to be realised or not, enough has at least been done to give us a glimpse of an order of nature to whose mysteries physical science has never found a key.

But in fact my father had so little time to spare for psychical research that he can only have regarded it more or less as a hobby, in a different category perhaps from other occupations falling under the same heading, but a hobby all the same.

Photography and carpentering were other recreations of which he never tired ; there was little he could not make with tools and timber, and one room—generally in the basement—of every house in which we lived for any length of time was always fitted up as a workshop. There, with his bench and a large assortment of tools—of which he took great care—T. W. R. frequently found relief for his brain from more purely intellectual work ; and household repair bills were kept down at the same time.

Photography always fascinated him. He took it up first in 1893 when it was quite exceptional for any one other than a professional photographer to own a camera. Rolleston's was a rather clumsy-looking box-wood plate camera which had to be mounted on a telescopic tripod and focussed under a black velvet cloth. The lazy method of to-day which enables one to buy neat little rolls of film and hand them to a chemist to develop and print had not then been evolved. The amateur photographer of the nineties was obliged to have his own dark-room and developing and printing plant and, generally speaking, the production of results was a complicated business of red lights, vulcanite and china trays, bottles of hypo., printing frames, and all sorts of other paraphernalia.

Besides making pictures of his family and friends, many of which are included in this book, Rolleston's camera accompanied him on all his tours and his albums are full of really delightful pictures. It is not hard to deduce from many of them that one thing which attracted him very strongly was anything that connoted power or energy. The sea, the wild cliffs and rocks of Western Ireland—suggesting age-old upheavals of Nature—majestic old trees, a river in flood, a waterfall, anything in fact wherein strength and power were either visible or latent. He never sought power for himself ; if he had he would probably have gone into politics ; but he was always drawn irresistibly as a subject for a picture to any setting which suggested the existence at some time or other of powerful natural forces. The merely pretty did not attract him at all, though there are in his albums many photographs of very great beauty. Some of these are reproduced here as well as others of the kind he most enjoyed taking. The old ash trees at ' Glasshouse ', the beeches at ' Hollywood ', and some of the coast scenes are typical of his favourite subjects.

The ' Big Wind ' of February, 1903, which is still remembered for the havoc it wrought in Ireland, provided him with a photograph of the Shannon in flood at Limerick and of the wreckage of Mr. Pollock's Observatory at Stillorgan.

At the Silver Sands in County Wicklow T. W. R. took many lovely photographs when, as children, we made our annual picnic there. These glorious stretches of sand with their backing of cliffs and mysterious caves would be worth a fortune to any country less out-of-the-way than Ireland. I believe more people have now ' discovered ' them but in the nineties, when the red-letter day in our year was that of the expedition to the Silver Sands, there was never another soul to be seen from one end of them to the other.

Archery was another pastime which T. W. R. took up at one time with his usual zest, and under his guidance we all attained a certain proficiency. He was intensely interested too in botany. In a letter to Miss Angel Stopford Brooke in 1888, after referring to literary matters, he went on :

' And, as a kind of diversion from these occupations, I have taken up botany rather vigorously. Do you know anything of it ? Bentham's *British Flora* is the book to work by, a wonderful work indeed, for it contains a description of *every* British plant, and also a most clear and interesting account of the physiology of the vegetable world, and gives you ready means of identifying any specimen you may come across. I wonder if this study has ever interested you ; if not I am sure it would do so if you gave it the chance ; it gives a new zest to every walk one takes in the country and you, living within reach of the College Botanic Gardens, could pursue it with great advantage.'

Angel Brooke, whom her brother, Stopford Brooke, re-christened ' Diamond ' and who was to us always ' Aunt Di ', was a life-long friend and regular correspondent of my father's. She became my godmother and, I am glad to say, is still very vividly alive at the grand age of eighty-nine ; I had nearly written ' grand *old* age ' but in truth Aunt Di is as young to-day as ever. She and her two elder sisters, Cecilia and Honor, lived at the time the above letter was written and for many years afterwards in Herbert Street, Dublin, a few doors away from two of their brothers, General Edward Brooke, R.E., and William Brooke, Chief Clerk of the Court of Chancery of Ireland. Both houses, 11 and 14 Herbert Street, were as well known to us when we were children as our own house only ten minutes walk away.

My father's letter to Aunt Di shows that as usual he tried to infect others with the enthusiasm with which he always tackled anything that interested him. He was never selfish with his recreations but wanted others to derive pleasure from them too. But I am afraid his children must often have disappointed him ; our brains had not his keenness and retentiveness and his painstaking efforts to make us as know-ledgeable as himself, especially where botany was concerned, were largely failures.

One very useful study, however, to which he did introduce me personally was the memory-training system devised by Professor Loisette. Loisette was, I think, a Canadian, but where my father came across his little treatise I do not know. It fascinated him and it fascinated me and when later on I went to the *Britannia* as a Naval Cadet I astounded every one, including the instructors and myself, by the speed with which I learnt the Morse Code by the application of the Loisette system. This was due entirely to the daily half-hours my father and I used to spend with his book.

Father used to teach us Irish too and at one time it looked as if we might really know the language. At home we nearly always used Irish for words and sentences in common use and I still often find myself lapsing into the language for such phrases as ' Here it is ! ' if I've found something I've been looking for, ' Shut the door ', ' Good morning ', and I can also if necessary tell a Sassenach to go to the devil without his having the slightest idea what I'm talking about !

Rolleston's enthusiasms were in fact infectious ; he made them so and his efforts to initiate us into the many mysteries of which he was a master were never like lessons. He taught us to play chess, of which he was very fond, and here he was perhaps more successful with us than where botany was concerned. I find an entry in his diary for 1898 where he recorded that I beat him twice in succession, from which he deduced either that his brain must be giving way or that I must have been exceptionally cute.

Before shutting up his photograph albums there is one other picture to which I must refer. It is of ' Toby '. Rolleston loved cats ; the philosophic placidity of their lives and the calm impertinence with which they assume that anything they fancy is *ipso facto* there specially for them appealed to him strongly. Toby was an immense black animal with a white nose, white paws, and a privileged position in the house ; he outlived his owner and died of an old age whose exact extent I do not think any one really knew.

On the day of my father's death Toby knew something was very wrong with his world and he tried very hard to get into the dining-room where his friend and master was lying. Later he went quite wild for a time and wandered away by himself ; but he came back eventually to the chairs and sofas which he regarded as being just as much his property as any one else's.

IV

GERMANY

IT was for the main purpose of taking up the position of reviewer of current German literature for *The Times Literary Supplement* that T. W. Rolleston left Ireland in 1909. The offer of such work was of course a very great compliment and my father carried it on till the end of his life in 1920 ; his last review in fact—of Professor Hume Brown's and Lord Haldane's *Life of Goethe*—appeared four days after his death.

Rolleston's connection with Germany and German literature and philosophy began at an early, though not very early, age. It was in 1879 that he married my mother, Edith de Burgh, and, as she suffered greatly from rheumatism, they lived in Germany, mainly at Wiesbaden—for the waters—and Dresden. Both my elder brothers were born in Dresden and spoke German almost before they spoke English.

It would have been quite foreign to a man of my father's character and temperament to live in a foreign country and be unable to speak its language ; so, lacking possibly the resources that would have enabled him to employ a teacher but being possessed of an amazing memory, he set out to learn it by himself. This he did by the straightforward but herculean method of buying a good German book containing plenty of dialogue and writing it out into English with the aid of a dictionary. When that had been done he was sufficiently well equipped to be able to publish, in collaboration with S. K. Knortz, a complete translation into German of Walt Whitman's *Leaves of Grass*. This, which appeared in 1880 when Rolleston was twenty-three years of age, was called *Grashalme* and echoes an admiration for the work of the great American poet which dated back to at least 1876 when my father was an undergraduate at Trinity College, Dublin. Though he never met Walt Whitman, who died in 1892, he had a considerable amount of correspondence with him and at least one letter from Whitman, written in 1879, survives. One of many earlier letters seems to have been given to Douglas Hyde for the sake of the autograph.[1]

A good deal later, in 1889, there also appeared Rolleston's *Life of Gotthold Ephraim Lessing* in the ' Great Writers ' series published by Walter Scott of London, and the year after saw the issue of *Lessing and Modern German Literature*. There was also, with H. B. Cotterill, his *Weber Wordsworth und Walt Whitman*, a 68-page reprint of lectures delivered before a Literary Society in Dresden.

Quite apart from the intrinsic value of these publications their appearance must be regarded as somewhat of an achievement when it is remembered that, as far as the German language was concerned, Rolleston left College with practically no knowledge at all. But in spite of that he became one of England's leading authorities on German writings and philosophy and occupied for eleven years the distinguished and important position already mentioned on the staff of the world's greatest newspaper.

Lessing, who lived from 1729 to 1781, is not often heard of to-day—at least not in this country—but the mark he left on German culture and thought is ineradicable and he lived in a time when living at all was a perpetual adventure. I cannot at this point refrain from quoting one of the concluding paragraphs of my father's life of this great German partly because what he wrote of Lessing might well be written of himself to-day :

No question left Lessing's hands without having been visibly advanced ; and wherever he laboured he laboured with the noble strenuousness and piety of one to whom every place is sacred that Truth inhabits. We may well say of him, as he said of Leibnitz, that his great manner of thinking, apart from the positive conclusions he supported, would alone have been an influence of the deepest value for his day and land.

T. W. Rolleston in fact made good use of the four years he spent in Germany at that period—1879 to 1883—and the knowledge he acquired was to stand him in good stead later on, particularly when in 1897 he was commissioned to make a tour of German schools and report on them and their organisation and methods for the Irish Commissioners of Manual Instruction. What he saw and learnt during that

[1] See letter to Hyde on p. 51.

tour only served to add to his admiration for many aspects of German life, and particularly for the thoroughness with which the German nation attacked any problem or under-taking to which it had set its mind and hand.

During this early residence in Germany we find Rolleston also contributing to the symposium of verse translations emanating three times a year from Trinity College under the name 'Kottabos' and with J. B. Bury, afterwards Professor Bury, a Fellow of T.C.D., as Editor. One of these translations *From the German of Uhland* suggests that Rolleston saw a spirit and inspiration in the Norse or German Saga very closely akin to those of the Celtic myths. There is at any rate a distinct Gaelic flavour about this, which is taken from *Kottabos*, Hilary Term, 1882 :

> King Siegfrid sat in his banqueting-hall ;
>   ' Who sings the best song of my harpers all ? '
> With harp in hand and sword on thigh,
>   A youth sprang out from the minstrelsy.
>
> ' Three songs I know, and O the first song,
>   I doubt thou hast forgotten it long :
> Thou hast my brother most foully slain !
>   And ever : thou hast him foully slain !
>
> ' The second song in my brain took form
>   In a night of darkness, a night of storm :
> Thou must fight with me, Siegfrid, for life and death !
>   And ever : must fight me for life and death ! '
>
> Then against the table his harp he leant,
>   And they drew their swords with a hasty hent ;
> And long they fought while the high hall rang,
>   Till the King sank down, and the minstrel sang :
>
> ' Now sing I the third and the sweetest song,
>   That to sing for ever I think not long :
> King Siegfrid lies in his crimson blood !
>   And ever : he lies in his crimson blood.'

If Rolleston had a high regard for Germany and for her contributions to literature, philosophy, and science it may be confidently stated that the feeling was reciprocated. He was held in very high esteem indeed in the Fatherland, and in fact a distinguished German engineer whose acquaintance I made not long before the war, told me, when he had learnt my name and that I was a son of T. W. R., that my father was 'the only Englishman for whom the Germans had any respect or regard'. But perhaps a greater tribute was that paid by the writer of a letter which appeared anonymously in *The Times* on 30 December 1920 :

It was by the merest chance I came across the letter about 'T. W. Rolleston' in your issue of December 16th. It is just about forty years ago now that he and I were very good friends, when I was a German student and he was living at Dresden. I used to come now and then from Leipzig to Dresden, at the invitation of some of my fellow students : and on such occasions I always took the opportunity of spending a few hours in Rolleston's company after I had had the honour and pleasure of making his acquaintance.

I had the good fortune to hear him deliver two addresses to a small and select German Literary Society, of which he was a member. His subjects were the poetical works of Wordsworth and Walt Whitman, and I have never heard a non-German speak the German language so eloquently or with such complete mastery. The Society got a limited number of these addresses printed, and I still have got my own copy.

We visited the battlefields round Dresden, and studied the battles of Frederick the Great and Napoleon, using as our text-books the historical works of Carlyle, Archenholz, Alison, and Thiers. Coming back one afternoon from Kulm to Dresden, we happened to meet Albert, King of Saxony, who was walking by himself near the Gross-Garten. He talked with us for nearly a full hour ; and in that time Rolleston got him to tell us something about the Sadowa and Gravelotte campaigns. The King was evidently surprised to see two young strangers taking such an interest in the military history of Germany, especially when we told him that we were not going to follow the military profession.

Rolleston and myself and some of our German friends were then very much interested in Draper's well-known work, *The Conflict between Religion and Science*, and the Literary Society discussed it on a few occasions. Rolleston made me a present of his copy of the work with some remarks of his own written into it, and he also gave me Matthew Arnold's *Literature and Dogma* at the same time. Both of these books I have still.

I have never known a man with a broader mind and bigger heart than T. W. Rolleston. His mind was full of the best and purest charity. I verily believe that if he heard the devil himself being abused he would have found something good to say for him. I have never met any man for whom I have had a deeper respect or higher admiration, nor one more worthy to be called 'a gentleman and scholar'.

'PACE'.

That such a tribute could have been penned by a German, one of our late enemies, only two years after the end of the Great War not only guarantees its sincerity but adds to its eloquence. The letter of December 16th to which 'Pace'

8

refers was written by the late Cloudesley Brereton and contained similar expressions of appreciation. I have never heard
who ' Pace ' was, but feel that it should be pointed out that
his memory failed him on one point ; it was Cotterill who
lectured on Wordsworth, Rolleston on Whitman.

The reader may have hitherto formed the impression that
my father was solely a scholar ; except for Standish O'Grady's
reference to the wood-chopping episode on page 28, little
mention has been made of his love of the open air and exercise.
This subject will recur, but the moment seems opportune for
stating that as a young man he was a keen Rugby footballer.
Rugby is of course the only kind of football that Irishmen
deem worthy of the name and St. Columba's College has given
Ireland, besides men of outstanding distinction in the world
of letters, many first-class players of the great game and many
Internationals. T. W. R., though not a front-rank player, was
a keen enthusiast and actually made an attempt, at about the
period being dealt with, to introduce the game to Germany.
That, I think, was in Dresden, and I have many times heard
him tell the story of how he got a couple of teams together,
borrowed or took possession of an open space somewhere, but
had to abandon the first game because the police thought it
looked too much like a free fight and too little like a game !
This, I believe, was the first game of Rugby ever played in
Germany.

Some of my father's book reviews done for *The Times* between 1909 and 1920 are still of considerable interest, especially in view of the fact that they covered the war period and
the five years preceding it. In July, 1909, there appeared for
example Herr von Bliebtreu's *Germany and England*, a book
which Rolleston described as ' a sincere contribution towards
a better understanding between the two countries.' After
quoting the author's statement that ' the Englishman and the
German are more closely related to each other than are any
two nations on earth ', Rolleston goes on to say that, despite
this natural affinity, there were at that time no two countries
which regarded each other with so much suspicion and ani-
mosity. According to Bliebtreu the picture of England as
seen through uninformed German eyes—perhaps one should
say ' misinformed '—shows the Englishman as ' the incarna-

tion of selfish arrogance and vainglory, inordinately proud of a history in which his success has been largely fortuitous, a shopkeeper with his eye bent fixedly on the main chance, and only now and then throwing up by some unaccountable accident a fiery genius like Shakespeare or Byron, who stands out brilliantly against a background of petty materialistic minds, devoid of all sense of the ideal.' Then follows— Bliebtreu is still painting the popular German picture—the particularly interesting opinion that ' the (British) Army is a laughing-stock, only fit to be clapped into prison if it showed itself on German soil ; the Fleet, undermanned and wretchedly constructed, is being rapidly outstripped by the young Marine of Germany.'

These were not entirely Bliebtreu's opinions but those of the general run of German people ; in view of the facts of history as relating to the achievements of the British Navy and Army prior to 1909 they can only have gained currency by reason of a studied and widespread campaign in Germany to pervert those facts. A whole nation cannot form such opinions unless they have been systematically educated to hold them—through their Press or other media.

Though Bliebtreu sets out, as Rolleston shows, to demolish this fantastic conception of England, it is interesting that he did agree, broadly speaking, with his countrymen's opinion of the British Army. Rolleston writes in his review : ' Nor will any German reader of this book easily delude himself with the idea that this once mighty power (England) is now exhausted and the Titan grown too weary for the burden. According to von Bliebtreu England could not, indeed, play a serious part at present in a land war on the Continent.' Almost exactly five years later the English Army was writing its ' contemptible ' name in heroic letters on the pages of European history, had halted German ambitions on the fields of Flanders, and had actually decided the outcome of the greatest war in history. Nine years after the publication of Bliebtreu's warning to Germany the British Army was policing a large portion of the country whose people in 1909 regarded that Army as ' only fit to be clapped into prison if it showed itself on German soil '.

Rolleston's own deep regret that Anglo-German relations should have deteriorated so badly is evident in the concluding

sentence of this review : ' It is eminently a book of the day ;
it is full of points of great, immediate, and practical interest
and it is worthy of careful reading by every one who laments
that there is something amiss in our relations with the ancient
and noble Teutonic stock from which our own nationality has
mainly sprung.'

V

THE WAR PERIOD

WHEN the war broke out in 1914 there is no doubt that
my father, whose contacts with Germany and things
German had been practically continuous for thirty-five years,
was personally very distressed that, if there had to be a war,
Germany and England should be on opposing sides. Apart,
however, from any personal regard he felt for his many German
friends and despite his respect for German achievements in
science, education, philosophy, and literature, he felt, even in
December, 1914, that we might be on the losing side. He
did not—and this opinion was shared by thousands of others
—have any very high opinion of the staying power of the
French, and I remember his saying to me at that time, even
when Paris had been saved and the Battle of the Marne and
Retreat from Mons had become history, that 'I'm afraid
we've backed the wrong horse.' Later, like others, he changed
that opinion, though at that time he would have ridiculed the
suggestion that the Defence of Verdun, for example, would
become a monument to French heroism and tenacity.

Nevertheless Rolleston did not permit his personal opinions,
inclinations, or feelings to affect his appreciation of the fact
that, between 1914 and 1918, the first duty of every British
citizen was owed to his own country ; and he had never been
slow to translate duty into action. If in the early days he had
visualised a war of short duration that would have been because he foresaw a swift German victory ; when that did not
materialise he realised, in common with others, that, before it
was over, every man, woman, and child in the Empire would
be required to play a part in striving for the victory that the
Marne and Mons had at least brought within the category of
things that might be hoped for.

What could he do himself ? He was fifty-seven years of age
in 1914 and had spent his life in a literary, artistic, and philo-

sophic atmosphere ; of war he knew nothing, though Douglas Hyde wrote of him that he ' really had an " imperial " mind. He loved armaments and soldiers marching and drums and music.' A Recruiting Officer might well smile if a would-be soldier were to put forward such qualifications as fitting him for a military career, but yet I find the following entry, dated Sunday, 4 October 1914, in the diary my father kept inter-mittently at that time :

After lunch I rode (cycled) to Wembley Park where the Old Boys Corps is drilling—saw Oliver Onions, Seton, and others, and decided to be enrolled. Then, three days later, I attended to-day my first drill in Regent's Park as a member of the Old Boys Corps. Very amusing and useful.

From then on the diary is an almost continuous record of drills and route marches, interspersed with references to other and more literary activities. Here are some typical entries :

Saturday, October 10th. Went to Wembley Park for drill in the afternoon and we had a severe time of it. To-morrow it begins at 9.45 and goes on I believe all day. There were about 700 on the field to-day.

Sunday, October 11th. Paraded 9.45. Cheery day. Drilling like any-thing except for two hours break for dinner, smoke, and chat. Fell in with D Company.

Saturday, October 17th. We fell in at Baker Street Drill Hall at 2 o'clock, started about 2.10, and reached Wembley Park 4.17—about 7 and three-quarter miles, which was considered a very good performance. About 800 strong. Then drill and home in the evening.

Sunday, October 25th. Fairly fine in the morning when I went to drill, but it came on to rain after lunch and we dismissed after tea. A good day as far as drill was concerned, as D Company seems to be getting the hang of things now.

But mere drilling and route marching were not enough ; there was real work to be done :

Friday, October 30th. I volunteered yesterday to help with erecting huts at Wembley Park and got there at 10.30 ; heavy work, shifting and sawing railway sleepers as foundations for six railway carriages which are to constitute the huts.

Wednesday, November 4th. I had volunteered for fatigue duty at the camp and went there early this morning, helping with the putting up of bunks in railway carriages.

The Old Boys Corps, which was made up of men like T. W. Rolleston with stout hearts, no illusions about ' playing at soldiers ', and a practical conception of the duty of a British citizen in those days when the news from the front seemed to pile horror on calamity and tragedy on disaster, was not then an official organisation, but on Friday, November 30th, we find that ' General Swayne told us we would shortly be " recognised " by the War Office.'

So the record of my father's attempt to help his country continues and, in September 1915, the diary records that ' I sent in to the Adjutant, Old Boys Corps, an offer to volunteer for entrenching work at the front.' This offer cannot have been accepted and the nearest my father got to actual warfare came when he was appointed to a machine-gun section and spent two or three nights per week on the roof of a city building, ready to open fire on raiding aircraft if the chance arose. That was after he had joined the Inns of Court Volunteers.

During this time Rolleston was also carrying on his literary and other work, though naturally public interest in German writings had disappeared and the opportunities for doing *Times* reviews were few and far between. There did appear, however, on 20 August 1914, a review of an English translation of some of the plays of Gerhart Hauptmann, and on 1 September a most interesting article on Heinrich von Treitschke.

This extraordinary individual, who was stone deaf,

' drew to the lecture hall of modern history in Berlin a dense throng, not only of students, but of soldiers, writers, officials—all the intellectual leadership of Germany ' ; and to such audiences Treitschke expounded his Gospel of Hate. ' So early as 1864 he had declared that " no European Power can be great without being great at sea ", and envy of England's sea power grew to be a kind of mania with him '. It is not in fact difficult to see in this Professor of History one of the most potent forces helping to form the average German's opinion of the English which Bliebtreu deplored and tried to correct. ' " With the English ", wrote Treitschke, " love of money has killed every sentiment of honour and every distinction between right and wrong, though they hide their poltroonery and their materialism under the unctuous phrases of religion." To overthrow such a power—or rather say such a lingering phantom of power—should be no difficult task for a virile people 60 millions strong—and then of what an inheritance to take possession ! '

In another place Rolleston wrote :

' Treitschke had at any rate no cant about him. He knew well what his programme involved and he taught his hearers that they must say farewell to a whole range of ideas once dear to the German heart. " That the strong should triumph over the weak," he declared, exactly in the spirit

of Nietzsche, " is an inexorable law of Nature." That the laws of civilisation are intended precisely for the purpose of enabling peoples numeri-
cally weak to develop their own life and culture in peace is a view which
cannot for a moment be allowed to check the career of German conquest.
" Why talk of founding Colonies ? " he once asked ; " Let us take Holland ;
then we shall have them ready-made." '

And yet people called Lord Roberts a scaremonger !

But in writing of German men of letters Rolleston was
clearly happiest when dealing with Goethe and Heine. Of
the latter he wrote in 1910—and some of this extract reads
very interestingly to-day when Hitler reigns supreme in the
Fatherland—while reviewing Gilbert Cannan's translation of
Heine's Memoirs :

The world has by no means done with Heine—his charm is true and
enduring. Many years ago the writer, like, no doubt, many another
student before and after, entered the realm of German literature through
the rose-wreathed gateway of the *Buch der Lieder*. And now, as one turns
over these pages in which is the soul of Heine, the perfume of true poetry
still rises from them. A master of verbal felicities, of poignant cadences,
of strange and splendid imagery. Heine might easily have become the
slave of his own endowments and have sunk to be a mere peddler in poetic
sensations. But he had nobler and sterner ideals of literature, and he
had the stubborn Jewish will which held his genius fast to these through
good and ill report, through triumph and misery, to the end . . .

What Heine really desired and fought for was the liberation of man in
body and spirit. He strove to break up the crust of outworn dogmas and
traditions and selfish tyrannies, which in his day weighed upon the spirit
of the German people with an oppression hardly realisable by us. As a
Jew he had felt that oppression in its worst and heaviest form. At Frankfurt, when Heine was a boy, and until Napoleon appeared as a liberator,
no Jew might show himself in any park or pleasure-ground, no Jew might
leave his ghetto after four o'clock on Sunday afternoon, only twenty-four
Jews in Frankfurt might marry in a year. The visible existence in Germany of a cultivated, powerful, and successful race who were not Christian
was felt to be a menace to religion, and through religion to the State
which was bound up with it. This narrow conception of the welfare of
the State operated in a greater or less degree by petty prosecutions, censor-
ships, and restrictions of all kinds, not only against the Jew, but against
every man of independent thought. In making war against this state of
things . . . Heine, it must be admitted, wrote many things that deeply
affronted German national feeling—things hard to be forgiven, and not
forgiven to this day . . . Yet Heine was never at bottom anything but
a good German. ' If I have been guilty of excess in my indignation
against the old, official Germany, the mouldy land of the Philistines—
which, however, has produced no Goliath, and not a single great man—
everything that I have said has been cunningly represented so as to make

it appear that I was speaking of the real Germany, the great, mysterious, and, as it were, anonymous Germany of the German people, of the sleeping sovereign with whose sceptre and crown the monkeys play.'

Heine was most truly one of the makers of Germany. That that country produced him is one of its chief glories, one of its many claims on the sympathy and admiration of the modern world. It is time that he were better understood there ; and to be understood is pre-eminently in Heine's case to be forgiven.

Of Goethe Rolleston wrote in the last article he penned for *The Times Literary Supplement* of 9 December 1920 :

Goethe remains a towering figure in European literature, the voice of a whole epoch . . . Evidently he had something to teach or proclaim which the modern spirit, in spite of all that is repugnant to it, feels to be congenial, to be consonant with its deepest needs and aspirations ; and he must have taught it surpassingly well. Is it possible in a few words to express the essential meaning of what Goethe was and is to the world of his day and ours ?

First we should say that in an age when the stream of European culture came to its broadest, fullest flood, and just before it split up into a hundred rivulets, each wandering out of sight on its lonely way, Goethe was the supreme embodiment of culture. He was not a scholar in any department of learning, but the range of his knowledge was immense, and all that he knew he knew vitally and made his own. Culture does not mean knowing things with the analytic intellect, but knowing them and having the habit of seeing and judging them in relation to other things, other branches of knowledge, other manifestations of life. Whoever has not this habit of seeing things in their relations—though he has as many languages as Mezzofanti and as much science as Newton—has not culture.

But Goethe had this pre-eminently ; through all his mature work one feels that there is not a quatrain or a sentence but comes out of a totality of thought and conviction, a vision of the world, in which he has organically part. His conversation, as reported by the admirable Eckermann, has the same quality. Every new fact or impression he felt he must bring into relation with the rest of knowledge or of sentiment, for only thus could it become alive and fruitful. Few have ever had this synthetising impulse as Goethe had it ; few have had his imaginative faculty, or the spontaneous, natural, literary gift which enabled him to express his discoveries in life ; few have had such a range of knowledge to co-ordinate ; none but Goethe has ever in equal measure united all three. He was the great master of culture, the greatest exponent of its methods and principles, at a time when culture was rapidly taking the place of religion as the guide of human life.

But Goethe had a religion too, though he did not call it so ; he had a gospel to preach which appealed, as it must always appeal, to the best minds in all ages. It was the gospel of service. He not only preached it, he most faithfully obeyed it. When he went to Weimar, he, a poet, sensitive, capricious, with wild forces for ever seething in his breast, bent himself to a long, toilsome, and often apparently hopeless performance of plain, practical tasks. As Minister—the word ' Vizier ' would express it better—of the little State, he reorganised its finances, forcing his Sovereign to economise and the nobles to submit to taxation ; he built roads and bridges, made canals, planted schools, raised the condition of the poor, and gave the peasants an interest in their lands. All this and much more was done with punctilious method, in the face of exasperating difficulties, through years of labour ; and, when he began it, he might have seemed one of the last men in Germany of whom this devotion to irksome duties could have been expected.

But there was a chord of bronze in Goethe's lyre, and it resounds again and again through all his poetry and prose. We have it . . . when he wrote to a certain luckless and rather worthless protégé : ' *Must* is hard, but it is only when a man *must* that his real inner nature is revealed. Anyone can follow his caprices ', or finally when he conceived the moment of highest bliss to have come for Faust in the thought of the redemption of a great tract of inundated land to be a home for men and the scene of happy and fruitful toil.

During the war period, however, Rolleston used his knowledge of the German and other languages for different and perhaps more practical purposes—though at first he does not seem to have thought they were of much value. He made the following entry in his diary under 25 January 1915 :

I went this morning to the War Office and found Mr. George Elder in Room 226, who told me I would be recommended for employment in the Censorship Department at £5 a week and asked me to get three letters of recommendation. I wrote for these to Dr. Gwynn, Professor Ridgeway, and G. W. Prothero.

Then, on February 15 :

I took up my work for the War Office, censoring letters at Salisbury House. Quite interesting job, but of very dubious utility, I fear. I read 46 letters, mostly Italian, and found nothing whatever to notice.

Besides reading German, Italian, and, I think, French correspondence my father also had a desk in the Obscure Languages Section of the Censor's office where he examined letters written in Irish. Although naturally this work was of a confidential nature, no details of it appearing in my father's diary, it seems possible that he may have revised his opinion of its value. At any rate Douglas Hyde wrote in the same letter in which he refers to Rolleston's love of drums and music :

I was very fond of him and had far more in common with him than I had with any of my other associates. I have spoken, I hope nicely, about

him in a book called *The League* [1] *and my Relation to it* in Irish . . . Some-
one who read the proofs reproved me, for he said that ' Mr. Rolleston was
employed by the Government to read letters in Irish during the Great War,
and he got Father '—somebody whose name I forget—' and his monastery
into great trouble.'

Whether or not there is any foundation for this story I do
not know and naturally my father left no record of it. What
may be taken for granted, however, is that, if the monastery
in question really did get into trouble through any report that
may have been made by Rolleston, then it deserved to do so.

At a later stage during the war T. W. Rolleston was associated with Count Gleichen and Mr. John Buchan—now Lord
Tweedsmuir—in the formation of the now forgotten ' Department of Information '. This organisation was not originally
intended to be of actual value during the war ; those who
promoted the idea saw that, when the hostilities had terminated, there would have to be made an organised endeavour
to re-establish trading relations with other parts of the world
and that the inevitable slump following the cessation of war
work would continue till factories—and industry in general—
had again picked up the threads of commerce. Millions of
men during that period would be laying down the sword and
finding neither pen nor ploughshare for them to use and one
of the obvious remedies for the widespread unemployment that
must result would be emigration. Men and women of all
kinds and classes would want to know where they had best
go and where there was a demand or opening for people with
their own particular qualifications ; traders and business men
also would be glad of reliable information as to where in the
Dominions, Colonies, or foreign countries there existed opportunities for re-establishing the export trade of the country
which the war had of course killed.

The Department of Information set out to collect the required
data, to establish a reference library in which both business
people and would-be emigrants would find what they wanted,
and to get together a nucleus staff which would make itself
as familiar as possible with the information—necessarily of a
very varied character—which they would be called upon to
provide.

[1] The Gaelic League.

It was an excellent idea, this ' get-ready-for-settling-down-again-after-the-war ' organisation and, before the Department's character had been changed and its energies diverted into other channels, a very fine and useful library had been collected and a system had been established that was capable of infinite expansion when the need should arise. T. W. Rolleston was the Librarian and was very enthusiastic, not only at having such very congenial work to do, but because he saw an exceedingly useful peace-time future before the organisation he had helped to create.

What particular factors then operated in the matter I do not know, nor exactly how the change in the Department's character came about, but change it did, till eventually it became a Department of Propaganda with the late Lord Northcliffe in command ; it was also given the status of a Ministry—the Ministry of Information. Its business thereafter was to keep an eye on the foreign and American Press and other publications and to take whatever steps might commend themselves to counteract any reports or statements that were injurious to the Allied cause.

In at least one direction the Ministry itself entered the field of propaganda and I remember my father telling me on one occasion, when I was on leave, that he had arranged for the translation of ' Bartimeus' ' excellent book, *Naval Occasions*, into no less than fifteen foreign languages.

Rolleston himself translated at least one book by a German author into English ; this was in 1916 before, I think, the Department of Information had been brought into existence. The book in question was *Because I am a German*, by Hermann Fernau, who was already known as a writer of distinction and the author of a book, published before the war, on the democracy of France. Rolleston wrote an introduction to his translation of this book in which, while laying the blame for the war on ' Prussianism ', he was still able to see, beyond the thousand miles of steel and flame that straddled Europe a German people who were thinking what Fernau wrote. This introduction ends :

The book is prohibited in Germany, and Fernau's friends there are of necessity dumb, but what he says aloud many must silently think, and even in Germany thought cannot be wholly under police supervision. When the War is ended a new war will begin, waged, perhaps, with other weapons, perhaps partly with the same ; it will be a war for the making of a new Germany. The issue deserves to be closely watched by all civilised nations, for on that issue turns the question whether the immense forces embodied in the German nation are to be won for reason and humanity, or to remain as agents of destruction and demoralization in the hands that are wielding them to-day against all that civilization holds most sacred and most dear.

After the war there was an immediate demand for drastic economy in Government expenditure. This was of course quite right and proper and Members of Parliament clamoured for retrenchment. Among the organisations the war had brought into existence was the Ministry of Information and, its original post-war objective having been submerged by the propagandist purposes to which it had been put, its death sentence was pronounced. Rolleston, among others who realised that the time had at last come for their work to bear fruit, protested in every possible way against its being thrown to the wolves of false economy and in particular implored the Government to preserve the Library, if nothing else, even if it were to be handed over to another Department—the Foreign Office or Colonial Office for example. But it was no use ; the axe fell and the benefit of eighteen months of preparation for peace was thrown away.

The rather sketchy diary kept by my father between 1912 and 1915 contains at least two other echoes of the war which will bring back memories to many people in the British Isles.

Wednesday, October 15th. After supper Owen [1] told us he heard firing and, looking out of the stair window, we saw, in the long beam of a search-light just below the Pleiades, the silvery shape of a Zeppelin with shells bursting round it, and a dull thud-thud of the guns very far off. I saw two Zeppelins moving northwards. They were visible only for a few minutes. Our Parliament Hill gun did not seem to have come into action. The whole affair as far as we saw it passed off in twenty minutes or so.

Rolleston, however, would not have spent twenty minutes looking at an air raid out of a window for, in addition to his other activities, he had early been enrolled as a Special Constable and on such occasions was always on duty. He was living then at ' Ifield ', 16 Prince Arthur Road, Hampstead,

[1] See page 7.

and his post was at the near corner of Arkwright Road where my stepmother used to take out hot coffee to him during the long winter nights.

The other war echo dates back a little earlier—to October 1914 :

> Sad news of the fall of Antwerp, accompanied by the arrival of a Belgian refugee whom we are taking in—a young but very self-possessed little person of about 16 years of age—Fernande Proot, daughter of a large shopkeeper, or something like that, in Antwerp.

Fernande stayed for two years and became almost one of the family ; arrangements were made for her to have a free course, under a scheme introduced for the purpose, at the Polytechnic Institute, and eventually she returned to her own country where she obtained secretarial work in a Belgian bank. Fernande is now happily married but my stepmother still hears from her regularly ; she has never forgotten her temporary English home in Hampstead although twenty-three years have now elapsed since she left it.

In spite of his many activities directly and indirectly connected with the war, Rolleston also managed during that period to maintain his contact with the various literary and allied movements with which he was concerned. These included the Irish Literary Society, the India Society, the Irish Texts Society—of which he was a Member of Council—and also a proposed Irish Institute which did not materialise but which was to have been a ' comprehensive Irish organisation in London for the study and furtherance of Irish interests '.

In addition he wrote short histories of Germany and Ireland for Hutchinson's *History of the Nations* and contributed articles to the *Hibbert Journal*, the *Quarterly Review*, and many other publications. He was indeed a tireless man who imposed on his normal duty of earning money with which to bring up and educate a young family the additional duty of doing his utmost for his country in those dark days of war.

This brief review of the latter part of his life—1909 to 1920 —would be sadly deficient if it contained no more than the passing reference to the India Society which has already been made. Rolleston, having all his life been a seeker after and lover of knowledge, had read and deeply studied the works of philosophers of all nations and of all ages. His mastery of the

T. W. R. PLAYING THE ZITHER

HOLLYWOOD HOUSE, 1905

BEECHES AT HOLLYWOOD

French, German, and Italian languages had enabled him to read the writings of all the most noted poets and thinkers in their own languages ; it was impossible to do so without also touching on art and music. But such matters as these latter Rolleston treated more as pleasant recreations than as serious studies ; by which I mean that, though his artistic and musical appreciation was profound and was based on intimate knowledge, he never attempted to turn his store of information and his critical faculties to financial account in those fields of endeavour. He could, had he so desired, have been a leading critic of either art or music, but he preferred otherwise and so was able to look at a lovely picture or listen to beautiful music with a mind entirely divorced from material considerations.

While in Germany in the early eighties Rolleston had been much attracted by the sweet plaintiveness of the music of that peculiarly German instrument, the zither. He learnt to play it himself and kept up the accomplishment all his life. Many times in the evening when his brain was tired he would draw the velvet cover from his own zither, place it on its special table, which was made as a sounding board, and would fill the room with delightful melodies. He scored some of the old Irish airs for this instrument and played them repeatedly, the last time only a few days before his death. When he was playing I do not think he was ever really conscious that any one was listening ; he played to himself and seemed to be lost in the melody his fingers were drawing from the strings.

In the artistic field too he progressed far and used to turn out delightful pen-and-ink sketches with which he occasionally illustrated accounts of some of his tours and trips in Ireland and elsewhere. But he was mainly interested, I think, in art as applied to design, and when he lectured on the subject for the Irish Industries Association and the Department of Agriculture he was not merely passing on second-hand information gathered from books, but was showing people how to do things he could do himself. He delivered also several addresses on art and the evolution of design for the Royal Dublin Society and illustrated them with lantern slides made from designs drawn by himself.

It was inevitable that these philosophic and artistic accomplishments should have led Rolleston outside a purely European orbit.   The world contained other nations and races and cultures, older perhaps than those of the ancient Greeks, and to which civilisation owes much in the fields of philosophy and art.   So it is not surprising to find him, in 1910, founding, in conjunction with Sir William Rothenstein, Mr. Laurence Binyon, Mr. E. B. Havell, and others, the ' India Society of London '.   This Society was formed in ' the belief of a body of artists and students that the aesthetic culture of India, more particularly in the provinces of painting, sculpture, and music, had in it elements of beauty and interest which in Europe, and even in modern India, were too little understood and valued.'

My father's work for the India Society, which is still being carried on, is best described perhaps in the words of Haridah Das, F.R.S.L., F.R.Hist.S., who wrote this tribute on his death :

Mr. Rolleston was the guiding spirit of this Society after he became Secretary on the retirement of Mr. Fox-Strangways. His keen interest to promote its cause, broad sympathy, and wide knowledge of Indian thought and literature, made him an accomplished Secretary. The work of the Society was so near to his heart that he gave gratuitously the last years of his life to its development. He had many plans in his mind which he often expressed with enthusiasm to his friends. The King's speech on the opening of the School of Oriental Studies, in which it was declared that ' the ancient literature and the art of India are of unique interest in the history of human endeavour ', stirred his sympathies and imbued him with the idea of establishing a Lectureship in Indian Art at the School of Oriental Studies. He spared no pains to make his scheme successful by influencing the Indian notabilities and others who were interested in Indian art to contribute to the funds for the purpose.

His home at Hampstead was always a centre of hospitality. . . . His amiability and readiness to help his friends either in literary or other spheres were characteristic. Many writers on Oriental subjects found in Mr. Rolleston a friend in need in connection with the publication of their works. He gave such aid with the same devotion that he would bring to bear upon his own work. The present writer owes Mr. Rolleston a deep debt of gratitude for such assistance . . .

It is a sacred duty to perpetuate the memory of such a man, who, by his personal sagacity and practical example, can well be claimed as a friend of India, and the memory of such an exponent should not die. In the Report of the India Society issued December, 1920, and signed by the Chairman, Lord Carmichael, we read : ' Mr. Rolleston's wide sympathies and scholarship, his personal distinction and untiring courtesy, made him an ideal Secretary, and under his able administration the Society has enlarged the scope of its activities and has steadily increased its membership, despite the brake the war necessarily put upon its initiative. No one had the interests of Indian culture more at heart than Mr. Rolleston. His loss will be felt far beyond the limits of the India Society. But he regarded his work for us as specially important, and the Committee believe that, in carrying out the plans he himself hoped to bring to fruition, they will be setting up the most fitting tribute to his memory.'

There can be no finer tribute paid to Mr. Rolleston's work in connection with the India Society than this ; but it may perhaps be suggested as a fitting tribute to his worth that the Society should name the Lectureship on Indian Art at the School of Oriental Studies after him.

As the India Society is now a most important and influential organisation some account of how it came into existence will not be without interest. T. W. Rolleston, among others, attended on 4 February 1910, a meeting of the Society of Arts to hear Mr. E. B. Havell deliver an address on ' Art Administration in India '. Mr. Havell criticised the trend of art education in that country, which, he pleaded, should be based on its own art traditions and not on schools and forms of comparatively recent European origin.

All this was perfectly in order and no doubt Mr. Havell's strictures were justified. It was the Chairman of the meeting, Sir George Birdwood, whose remarks led a number of those who were present to publish, in the form of a letter to *The Times*—which appeared on February 28, a strong protest against those remarks and to convene a meeting, held at Mr. Havell's house, at which the India Society came into existence.

Sir George Birdwood's remarks which produced this result had concluded as follows—he was commenting on examples of Indian art which Mr. Havell had exhibited :

My attention is drawn to the photograph on my left of an image of the Buddha as an example of Indian ' fine art '. This senseless similitude, in its immemorial fixed pose, is nothing more than an uninspired brazen image, vacuously squinting down its nose to its thumbs, knees, and toes. A boiled suet pudding would serve equally well as a symbol for passionless purity and serenity of soul.

In *The Times* letter the signatories, after quoting these remarks, went on to say :

We recognize in the Buddha type of sacred figure one of the great artistic inspirations of the world. We hold that the existence of a distinct, a potent, and a living tradition of art is a possession of priceless value to the Indian people, and one which they, and all who admire and respect their achievements in this field, ought to guard with the utmost reverence

9

and love. While opposed to the mechanical stereotyping of particular traditional forms, we consider that it is only in organic development from the national art of the past that the path of true progress is to be found. Confident that we here speak for a very large body of qualified European opinion, we wish to assure our brother craftsmen and students in India that the school of national art in that country, which is still showing its vitality and its capacity for the interpretation of Indian life and thought, will never fail to command our admiration and sympathy so long as it remains true to itself. We trust that, while not disdaining to accept whatever can be wholesomely assimilated from foreign sources, it will jealously preserve the individual character which is an outgrowth of the history and physical conditions of the country, as well as of those ancient and profound religious conceptions which are the glory of India and of all the Eastern world.

This letter was signed by thirteen distinguished artists and writers and the following comprised the first Executive Committee of the Society, with Sir William Rothenstein as Chairman : Professor T. W. Arnold, Mrs. Leighton Cleather, Dr. Ananda Coomaraswamy, Mr. Walter Crane, Mr. E. B. Havell, Mrs. (afterwards Lady) Herringham, Dr. Paira Mall, and Mr. T. W. Rolleston, who was Honorary Secretary and Treasurer.

It is not too easy to deduce from these facts who was the founder of the Society, if indeed that distinction can be claimed for any one individual. My father drafted the letter to *The Times* and the idea of a Society—the kind of medium he always favoured for the purpose of furthering any objective of the sort—may have then been in his mind. But Mr. Havell presumably convened the meeting held at his house. Haridah Das definitely points to Rolleston when he writes that he founded the Society *in conjunction with* Sir W. Rothenstein, Mr. Laurence Binyon, Dr. T. W. Arnold, Mr. E. B. Havell, and others.

At any rate the Society lost no time in getting to work and it stands to its everlasting credit that Sir Rabindranath Tagore's now world-famous *Gitánjali*, and his lovely drama, *Chitra*, were first published in English by the India Society. Four years after its foundation it was also embarking on ' the publication of a series of over fifty plates and engravings representing in colour and monochrome Lady Herringham's full-scale copies of frescoes in the Buddhist cave-temples at Ajanta.' Works dealing with Mughal and Rajput drawings and with *Music in Hindustan* were also published before the end of 1914 and in general the Society pursued with energy its object of making the aesthetic culture of India better known and appreciated in the West.

The Rolleston Memorial Lecture suggested by Haridah Das was delivered in the Lecture Hall of the Victoria and Albert Museum on 2 January 1922 by Professor Strzygowski, whose subject was 'Indo-Persian Landscape Painting and Northern India'. Laurence Binyon, LL.D., was in the Chair.

VI

SINN FEIN

IN spite of his devotion to the many other interests already mentioned it would be a grave mistake to suppose that my father's departure from Ireland in 1909 involved any reduction in his concern for the condition of his native land. Though no longer on the spot and unable therefore to take a very active part in Irish matters he continued to contribute frequent articles on the ever-changing situation to a number of journals and reviews. These included the *Westminster Gazette, Daily Telegraph, Land and Water, National Weekly, Observer, Oxford Magazine, Nineteenth Century*, and *Times*, and in addition he published two pamphlets, ' Ireland and Poland : a Comparison ', and ' Ireland's Vanishing Opportunity ' in 1917 and 1919 respectively.[1]

In all these writings Rolleston's objective was to put the Irish position as plainly and fairly as possible before the world and, as the period was a most important—not to say revolutionary—one in Irish affairs it will be of interest to deduce from them what his attitude was towards the Sinn Fein movement, the Third Home Rule Bill—which would have led to Civil War if a greater war had not supervened—the Easter Rising of 1916, the Irish Convention, and the situation after the Great War had ended. He did not live to see the Treaty of 1921 signed nor the advent to power of Mr. de Valera and his Republic.

Sinn Fein, which means ' Ourselves Alone ', originated with the late Arthur Griffith who, in 1904 in a pamphlet called ' The Resurrection of Hungary ', advocated for Ireland a policy of passive resistance to and abstention from co-operation of any kind with England in the management of Irish affairs. The main factor in the then situation was that

---

[1] Both published by T. Fisher Unwin, Ltd., and the second also by the Talbot Press, Ltd., of Dublin.

a large number of Irishmen—besides those, like my father, with whom the belief was at least twenty years old—had at last come to the conclusion that the regeneration and revival of Ireland would not come through the agency of the Irish Members at Westminster. It was not the fault of Griffith that the Sinn Fein movement later got out of hand and turned to violence, culminating in the Easter Rising ; so, in its early days it received the whole-hearted approval of many who had already spent several years planting and nursing the co-operative movement in industry and agriculture.

What Rolleston thought about it is well summarised in the following letter written to Lady Aberdeen on 5 September 1906 ; this was a few months after Lord Aberdeen had commenced his third term as Lord-Lieutenant of Ireland.

DEAR LADY ABERDEEN,

I wrote to you lately about recent developments in the Gaelic League, and as you were interested in what I told you, I feel inclined to inflict another letter on Irish affairs on you and His Excellency. You must have noticed that public affairs in Ireland wear a very different look from that which they bore when you were here last. There are more reality, more freedom, more practicality, in Irish thought and action than there used to be. But these good qualities are often associated with what is called the Sinn Fein, or ' intransigeant ', view of politics. This is a phenomenon by no means without danger, direct and indirect, to the progress of Ireland. It is of course a relic from the old Fenianism, but in a way, it is worse than Fenianism. It does not, for the present at all events, contemplate serious action, as Fenianism did, but it throws itself all the more vigorously into the mission of influencing thought. With acute insight its leaders have perceived the use the Gaelic League can be to them in this direction, and they have accordingly identified their cause as much as they possibly can with the cause of the Gaelic League and have practically gained control of its official organ, and have more or less terrorised the Executive Committee.

A recent novel by Miss Mary Butler, called *The Ring of Day*, embodies very much the ideas of the Sinn Fein party. She asked me to review her book in the *Evening Mail*. I did so, and enclose you what I wrote. I send also her letter to me after reading the review. You see she is open-minded and friendly—nothing bitter about her, no intolerance of frank criticism ; but there is no wavering about her convictions. The strength of these people lies in the fact that they have more sincerity, more high-mindedness, more principle, and very much more education and intellect, than any other section of the Nationalist party at present possesses. Hence their great and growing influence over all the active young minds now coming to maturity in Ireland. Young people are usually impassioned for ideas and for reason, when they have the education to grasp them. They are getting the education now, in Catholic and Nationalistic Ireland. They don't understand a Party which talks sedition in Ireland and America and takes the oath of allegiance at Westminster— which abuses the British Army and at the same time makes violent scenes in the House because Irish soldiers in it are not allowed to wear the shamrock—which denounces England's ' piratical ' wars, and tells her that Ireland will supply soldiers for them if only Home Rule is granted to her. This sort of thing disgusts them.

Another point of importance about them is this. They embody the rising force of resistance to clerical dictation in Ireland. The Bishops have reduced the Parliamentarians to mere puppets, but they have no influence at all over the Sinn Fein people, to whom a Bishop, when he is dealing with secular affairs, is no more sacrosanct than a Resident Magistrate. Therefore numbers of people, like Mr. Hannay,[1] for instance, support the Sinn Fein movement and add to its mass and momentum, simply because they see in it the one force in Ireland that can with any effect make head against the domination of the clerics. These people have courage and brains, and they have an organ which expresses their ideas with a slashing power, ——————— very well adapted to spread their ideas among the people. This paper you probably know—it used to be the *United Irishman* and was then financed by Miss Maud Gonne—it now bears the title *Sinn Fein* and . . . . and . . . . . are supposed to be its props, in the financial sense. It cannot do without such props, for advertisers fight a little shy of it.

[1] ' George Birmingham.'

The *Leader* gets the advertisements, but is now quite discredited among the rising generation and has, I am told, suffered very serious losses in circulation . . . .

The Sinn Fein men therefore hold the field among the political forces of the day. The one power which is in a position to challenge their leadership over the rising generation is the Church. It will assuredly do so in its own time and its own way. The Church has no idea at all of letting eighty Catholic votes disappear from a legislative assembly ruling one-fifth of the earth's surface, including some twelve million Catholics. That the Church would win if the fight came at the present moment there can be no doubt. It will probably win at any time, at least it will leave the Sinn Fein movement in possession of Dublin alone—it—the Church—is supreme in the rural parts of Ireland and Dublin does not lead Ireland as Paris leads France. Unhappily the victory is one which people like myself would have to look on with very mixed feelings ! Ireland needs a free and well-informed public opinion. It cannot have that as long as the Church holds its present position of unbounded authority over men's minds and is able to ruin any Catholic professional man or trader who opposes it. It will, I believe, beat Sinn Fein because Sinn Fein has the really weak point of extreme separatist views ; there it will attack and there it will win. But will it be a victory for enlightenment and progress ? Will it help to clear the stage for truer conceptions of Ireland's ideal ?

It might, in my opinion ; if only there were any party in Ireland conscious of such an ideal and able to use opportunities for preaching it. I long ago saw that the ideal feeling, the sense of principle and of logic which animates the Sinn Fein party could only be properly met by opposing to them, not mere utilitarian arguments, not the brute force either of the State or of ecclesiasticalism, but ideals as high as theirs and more practicable, a logic more in touch with realities. A victory of thought in fact, not a victory of force or authority, was what seemed to me supremely desirable. With this in view I wrote my pamphlet on Ireland and the Empire, and another paper which appeared in ' Dana '. That I was on the right track was evident from the fury with which the organ of the party fell upon me. They compared me rather unfavourably to Judas Iscariot, and have never ceased to vilify me by every sort of abuse, though of late I think my personal friends among the party have put some check upon this violence. Those who attacked me were, however, quite right in recognising that I must be discredited by fair means or foul. I had ideas that interfered with their monopoly and with the power they wielded. And it is curious to notice that, while they rather approved of Sir Horace Plunkett as long as they thought he was merely founding creameries, &c., the moment they perceived from his book that he had ideas too, they fell upon him tooth and nail. This is in a way encouraging. But I fear little progress has been made towards the formation of a party animated by these ideas and possessing an organ capable of giving expression to them. Perhaps if the organ could be brought into existence it might evoke the party—perhaps the scattered individuals who share these conceptions are more numerous than appears on the surface. At any rate I am sure the only way to move people's minds on any large scale is not by mere statement, but by reiteration, by shouting one's mind to them if necessary—by *singing* it if possible !—as the Young Irelanders did. And for all that a newspaper is the only thing. Something of the kind existed during the period when Sir Horace and T. P. Gill controlled the *Express* and it was doing good work. But a weekly paper would be better, and cheaper. If there were an intelligent millionaire who wanted to do a good stroke of work for Ireland, I think he would promptly found such a paper.

Sincerely yours,

T. W. ROLLESTON

But the Sinn Feiners went too far and, instead of confining their policy and the enthusiasm with which Arthur Griffith had succeeded in imbuing the whole of the South to internal organisation, they talked of setting up Consulates in foreign countries, of building merchant ships, of boycotting imports from England—as if England were not bound to retaliate—and more to the same effect. But any programme of self-sufficiency must of course place Sinn Fein in opposition to the Irish Members, who saw the conduct of Irish affairs in the political sphere—the only one about which they knew or cared anything—being taken out of their hands. Rolleston, in an article which appeared in the *North American Review* in February 1908, described the situation at that time as follows, referring first to the steps mentioned above :

Such is the programme of action which is running like a prairie fire among the young men who will shortly be shaping the policy of Ireland. Unless the Parliamentary movement can offer on its side a programme equally clear, honest, and self-consistent, it seems to me that it must inevitably go down before its antagonist. Young Ireland is now educated as it never was before, and is learning to think. It will not be content with a flabby opportunism which talks separatism in America, Imperialism in Australia, agrarianism in Connaught, and a self-reliant Nationalism nowhere. Parliamentarianism will be forced back on its first principles. It cannot afford to be nakedly opportunist and to scoff at principles any longer, as it did in the days when it had indeed *enemies* in Ireland, but no *rivals.*

In the same article Rolleston pointed out that the Irish Parliamentary Party was almost entirely financed by contributions from America ; he regarded these subsidies as inconsistent with a policy of ' Ourselves Alone ' and wrote very tellingly on the subject :

I wish earnestly to appeal to Irish-Americans, whose splendid generosity and fidelity have been so conspicuous in the history of the cause, to consider whether their very eagerness to help is not in part responsible for the situation of to-day. They have shifted the centre of gravity of the Irish movement from Ireland itself to another country. It cannot be good for any people to have their political work done for them at the expense of others. People who live in the United States cannot possibly, however great their sympathy, be in touch with the realities of Irish life. Yet they control the Irish situation, as the power of the purse always must. They can have no knowledge of most of the party whom they maintain ; they have no personal responsibility, whether we win or lose on the lines they dictate. Why not leave the movement to those who have that knowledge and that responsibility, and whose lives and fortunes are bound up with the future of their native land ? We have no need of American money —not a dollar of it. There was none forthcoming for O'Connell, but O'Connell maintained his long struggle, first for Emancipation, afterwards for Repeal, out of the resources of an Ireland much poorer than Ireland is at present. Ireland spends 70,000,000 dollars a year on alcohol and 17,000,000 on tobacco. An infinitesimal sacrifice of these luxuries—not to say poisons !—would yield the 100,000 dollars a year supposed to be necessary to carry on the struggle for our national existence. What justification then is there for laying the ends of the earth under periodic contributions for the furtherance of our cause ? The only effect is to foster a class of politicians independent of the people whose aspirations they are supposed to represent, and to relieve that people of the wholesome necessity of thinking and acting for themselves. Only let Ireland's friends in America cease these contributions, and they will immediately force these politicians in turn to their own people, and to frame a policy which that people approve and which that people will follow. By so doing Ireland's American friends will brace and tone up the whole movement. They will make the situation as full of health and hope as it is now of discouragement and demoralisation. They will put it at once on its proper basis : the centre of gravity will be restored to Ireland.

Rolleston in fact approved of the principles of ' Ourselves Alone ' provided the stress was put on ' Alone '. He saw in the movement the possibility of Ireland sending to Parliament a different set of politicians to replace those in whom he and others who thought with him had no sort of confidence at all.

But not long afterwards came another Home Rule Bill, and, as was bound to happen, Ulster began to arm ; so therefore did the South—under the Sinn Fein banner. The ' National Volunteers ' came into existence and started drilling in order to be ready to defend the Bill against Ulster. At about the same time—the summer of 1914—there was liaison with Germany, in which Sir Roger Casement and possibly Kuno Meyer acted as negotiators. There is no direct evidence that German money actually helped to finance the ' Republicans ', but it is beyond dispute that Germany was to play much the same part as France had played of old in Irish affairs.

Rolleston still adhered to the belief that properly co-ordinated, industrial, agricultural, and essentially non-political and voluntary organisations would provide Ireland's surest road to prosperity, and in fact said in a speech at Sheffield in 1915 that he could not help ' believing that these were the forces that were going to prevail in the long run.' The ' long run ' —still how distant !

Though at the beginning of the Great War both Ulster and the South shelved their own differences and the Home Rule Act was laid aside, the Sinn Feiners went too far and too fast ; impatience and German encouragement led to the Easter Rising and its subsequent tragic executions.

Rolleston pleaded urgently for an abandonment by the Revolutionaries and their hot-headed leaders of the disastrous course they had elected to follow, and pointed out that Ulster still stood in the way of the creation of a real Irish nation. This extract comes from an article in the *National Weekly* of 4 April 1917 :

The first and fundamental condition of any successful movement towards any kind of national self-government for Ireland is surely that it must carry the whole Irish people with it—not necessarily to the last man, or the last dog or cat, as the German Chancellor put it, but certainly not to the exclusion of great and weighty interests and sections of the Irish people. That is what the party of revolt constantly ignores. They ignore Ulster. Without Ulster there can be no Irish nation. But without an unqualified acceptance of the integrity of the Empire, Ireland cannot have Ulster. Were the Sinn Fein party to carry all the rest of Ireland with them they would still have to face this irremovable bar to the realisation of their fantastic ambitions. Everything they do and say tends to justify and stiffen the resistance of Ulster, not to separation alone—for that is already at the utmost height of intensity and resolve—but to any form of self-government which would give to disloyalty a new leverage for effective action. It is nothing short of amazing that men of the intelligence and sincerity of many of the Sinn Fein leaders should seem incapable of recognising a fact that really fills the whole horizon of Irish politics. They, who denounce the division of Ireland, are every day working with their own hands to make the gulf deeper and more impassable. That German agents with their usual callousness—the kind of callousness that proposed to hand over three American States to Mexico !—should encourage this attitude in Ireland is comprehensible enough. They make temporary trouble for England, and they know well that Germany will never be called upon to carry her programme into action. When once she has made Irishmen serve her turn, when they have filled their native land with all the violence and destruction that they are good for, she will fling them into the bloody mire like a broken gunwheel.

But that any Irishmen should lend themselves to be the tools of a policy so disastrous and impossible, so plainly anti-national and retrograde, is only to be accounted for by an utter incapacity for comprehending the large forces that are re-shaping the British Empire, and indeed the whole modern world. Within the framework of that Empire great and desirable changes are possible in the government and administration, not only of Ireland, but of the other sections of the United Kingdom. And on this basis the unity of Ireland—North and South—is at least a reasonable and practical aim. It is an aim which has never yet been clearly conceived and steadfastly pursued. Why not give it a trial ? But outside it no headway can ever be made, and in the genius, courage, and devotion given to a false ideal we see the most precious resource which Ireland possesses running irretrievably to waste.

Are we to go on for ever ploughing these barren sands ? Irish faculty does not run to waste like this in other countries. There is no Sinn Feinism in California, nor does Massachusetts, which is largely Irish and was once a sovereign State, look on incorporation in the American Union as a degradation of its ideals. The small States of Europe, which, when they are not actually trampled on, like Belgium, have to look on helplessly not even daring to utter a protest, when their peaceful citizens are lawlessly murdered on the high seas—does any of these present an Ideal for which Irishmen should wish to exchange their citizenship of the British Empire ? If the best and sanest minds in Great Britain and in Ireland would only unite at this critical hour to make that citizenship a reality for every class and for every race in the three Kingdoms, then indeed we should not have passed through these troubled days in vain.

I think the appalling degeneration of the Irish situation and the destruction of all the good work that he and Plunkett had been doing—work that must have resulted in bringing North and South gradually together—nearly broke my father's heart. He loved his country as only a few other men have done and it shocked and humiliated him to be a fellow-countryman of those who, apart from all other considerations, had so madly re-built and so stoutly re-fortified the barrier between North and South that had begun to show signs of crumbling.

Yet I think the major portion of the blame for the events of the last twenty-five years must be laid at the door of Ulster. If, instead of rushing to arms in opposition to the Third Home Rule Bill, the North had decided to help to make the new régime work we would probably never have heard of the Irish Republic. Ulster's clear duty to the England she professes to love so deeply—and to the Empire—was not to hold off her fellow-countrymen at the points of smuggled bayonets but to make a sacrifice—that might not have been a sacrifice at all—for the sake of curing the Anglo-Irish ailment which is still a disgrace to the British Empire. If, having put her shoulder to an all-Irish wheel, Ulster had subsequently found that her ' loyal ' citizens were expected to fall in with or subscribe to ' disloyal ' actions then would have been quite soon enough to talk about resistance by force.

Now of course the South must retrace its steps to the pre-war position ; the sign-post on the road to a real Irish settlement is still where it was when Parnell died and when the ' Self-help ' movements began ; the only possible course for Southern Ireland is to get back to the cross-roads where that sign-post stands and make a new start as an integral part of the United Kingdom. This will be putting herself in the right and the more Southern Ireland is in the right the more will

Ulster be in the wrong till she decides to co-operate. If Ulster would only contribute to make this possible, even by merely saying that she will maintain an attitude of benevolent neutrality, it would be a long step forward. But when the North starts objecting to a settlement before knowing whether its citizens are even to be asked to participate in it neither Ireland nor the Empire will get any further ahead—and in the end Ulster will be ruined too. England cannot go on allowing a handful of Northern industrialists to wreck every attempt to bring the ' long run ' to an end—provided the South decides to take the right and sensible road. Northern Ireland's General Election in February 1938 lost her ' loyal ' citizens a great deal of sympathy throughout the Empire—sympathy which she can only regain by co-operating instead of obstructing.

In 1917 came the Irish Convention presided over by Sir Horace Plunkett. Great things were hoped for from it ; all elements in all Ireland except unfortunately Sinn Fein, were represented, but the gathering's efforts proved abortive ; extremists on both sides were determined to wreck it ; and they did. There was an inability or a downright unwillingness to recognise that both sides must put something in the pool and must put up with the loss of something they had always professed to cherish if a compromise was to be reached. Some claims on both sides—North and South—would have had to be shelved for the moment, even if each party had made a mental reservation to put them forward again after a measure of co-operation had been achieved.

The chaos, therefore, that Cardinal Logue predicted as a consequence of any failure of the Convention reigned in Ireland—as it still does. Meantime a very distinguished Irishman, Lord French, had been sent to Ireland and sane Irishmen hoped his influence both in the North and South would be productive of good. But nothing came of these hopes and the British Government still avoided doing any of the obvious things that might have softened Irish tempers. The situation towards the end of 1918 is vividly described by Rolleston in a special interview which appeared in the *Observer* on 1 September :

Observer. May we ask you to tell the readers of the *Observer* what you think of the present Irish policy of the Government ?

Rolleston. Have they got a policy at last ? I wish to goodness you could tell me that ! I don't think I ever saw British opinion in all circles so anxious to do the right thing about Ireland, and yet so flurried and bewildered as to what that thing may be. Just look at the proposals that are constantly being put forward by the Government and by the Press ! Home Rule with conscription, Home Rule without conscription, conscription without Home Rule, Home Rule for all Ireland, Home Rule with partition—all sorts of ingenious plans for bringing Ulster under Home Rule and yet keeping the Irish Parliament from having any authority there ; and, when the problem proves insoluble on these lines, frantic appeals to Colonial Premiers, President Wilson, or God knows who, to think of something that has passed the wit of man in these islands ! There has never been anything like it, except the antics of the proverbial old gentleman plunging about the room to find the spectacles which are across his forehead.

Observer. Then you will do a great service if you can tell him where to find them. But the policy we had in our mind is none of these. It is the policy of economic development announced in Lord French's Belfast speech of August 5th.

Rolleston. Ah, that is quite another story ; and I am glad to see that the *Observer* has got its eye on this most striking pronouncement. But is it a policy ? Is the Government in earnest ? If so, then I should say with a good deal of conviction that Lord French has found the spectacles. If he, and the Premier, and Mr. Shortt really mean all they have said they will transform the whole Irish problem within the next seven years.

Observer. But after all that has been done for Ireland in this direction, and done in vain, doesn't that seem rather a large statement ?

Rolleston. Not at all. You are now, whether you realise it or not, making a wholly new departure. I don't for a moment deny the goodwill and the good statesmanship which have been shown by the reforms of the past generation. But, after all, you were, in the main, only doing what Ireland could and would have done for herself, and done much earlier, if she had had the power. You are now going to show Ireland that the Imperial connection is not a drag on her progress, but, on the contrary, that you are harnessing to that progress the strongest motive-power in the world to-day.

Most Englishmen imagine that Ireland is a kind of spoiled child on whom Great Britain has been lavishing benefits. She is nothing of the kind. For centuries she was the Cinderella of the three Kingdoms. I admit, and indeed I have elsewhere fully shown, that she is not an oppressed and downtrodden country like Prussian Poland, for instance. Yet even now she is far from having been accepted as one of the family. Look, for instance, at the splendid vista which Mr. Fisher's schemes are opening up to the cause of elementary education in Great Britain ! With what eyes do you suppose the Irish teacher, with his wretched pittance and his miserable equipment, looks on at all this ? We pay the same taxes as you do, but we are far from getting the same proportionate return of Imperial expenditure. In education, in expenditure on public services not directly connected with the maintenance of Imperial authority, in the apportionment of the Development Grant, in economic development generally, we are getting nothing like our rightful share of the common revenue. Since the outbreak of the war, Irish taxation has gone to swell the earnings of the British working-man, but of the Niagara of gold that has poured out in that direction, how much has come to Ireland ? Only the merest trickle. Why, even to-day, after Lord French's declaration, you are proposing to spend over a million in stimulating flax growing, and to spend it wholly in Great Britain ! It is on facts like these that the Sinn Fein movement lives and thrives. If you want to produce a better situation in Ireland you must radically alter this attitude of yours, and you must do it at once.

Observer. Let us come to details then. What exactly do you propose ?

Rolleston. It is as simple as A B C. Probably no policy pregnant with such great results is capable of being so definitely set forth, or carries with it so obviously its own credentials. In the first place, as recommended strongly by the Irish Railway Commission of 1906, the Government should buy up the Irish Railways, reduce freights, link up the various lines—I believe there are nearly thirty of them—run branches to the coal-fields and other mineral centres, and make the system a real economic service to the country. This need not cost the Government a sixpence : on the contrary, as has been shown in a useful pamphlet on the subject lately brought out by Vacher—' The Road to Irish Prosperity '—it would prove a great asset to the State.

Then a naval dockyard, with a port for trans-Atlantic traffic, should be established in one of the natural harbours of the West of Ireland, linked with a tunnel joining the Scottish and Irish coasts. The main drainage of the valleys of the Shannon and the Bann is a project which has waited far too long for execution ; it should be taken in hand at once. Waste lands should be taken for afforestation, compulsorily if necessary, and with no sort of tenderness in the way of fancy prices for sporting estates. Similarly land purchase, so unfortunately checked by the repeal of the Wyndham Act in 1909, should be pushed through to the end with com-pulsory powers. The Department of Agriculture should be made to abandon its ridiculous and mischievous objections to co-operation, and should proceed hand in hand with the Agricultural Organisation Society in developing rural life and business on co-operative lines, and so help in solving in the only possible way the serious problem of bringing a good proportion of the large grazing ranches under tillage. In regard to indus-tries other than agricultural, they will take care of themselves if the big, fundamental things outlined above are done. Irish manufacturers should, however, have better facilities and more fair play in competing for Govern-ment contracts. All this, of course, you will have to work through some new Body—a Board of Economic Development.

Finally, Irish elementary education should be taken seriously in hand ; teachers well trained and decently paid, schools, large and small, well equipped, and much more care taken in regard to the kind of teaching given at all schools in receipt of Government money. No plank of the new platform is more important than this, and in nothing has Ireland a more serious and well-founded grievance than in the starvation of her elementary school system as compared with England or Scotland.

Well, that is roughly the programme. There is hardly a feature in it —if there is even one—which has not behind it either some recent declaration of the Government, or the Report of a Commission, or some powerful body of highly qualified opinion. If carried through boldly and completely it will cost nothing ; on the contrary there will probably be a handsome balance to the good. In other than financial aspects, the gain would be altogether incalculable. You will have a genuine United Kingdom for the first time in history. You will buy out the fee simple of Irish sedition and discontent.

Observer. Don't you think that if it were possible to do that by such means as you describe we should have seen some signs of it after all that has been already done in the way of reform ?

Rolleston. And haven't we seen them ? Those of us who have watched Ireland closely for the past generation have seen nothing more remarkable and more hopeful than the outburst of patriotic feeling towards the Empire and its cause which took place in Ireland when war was declared. Irish national sentiment was never stronger than at that time, but it was becoming a strength, not a danger, to the Empire.[1] That was the reward of the policy of reform. Home Rule had nothing whatever to do with it. The response would have been still greater if that unlucky and most ill-devised measure had never been brought in. But Ireland's evil genius took charge at this point. Government went suddenly crazy and behaved as if it had set itself deliberately to manufacture sedition. And this brings me to the question which must cause the deepest anxiety to every loyal Irishman. Is that evil genius going to assert itself again ? Are the Viceroy's declarations mere words with no purpose or sincerity behind them ? Is this another case of what Sir Edward Carson so justly denounced as ' trifling with Ireland ' ? If so, I can only say that the result will be calamitous beyond expression. It will simply take all the heart and hope out of those who are working for the cause of Imperial loyalty in Ireland. It will kill that cause for as far into the future as any living man can see, and those who have allowed themselves to trifle with Ireland for some wretched object of political tactics will incur a terrible and a criminal responsibility.

If only the Government of the day—or any British Government at any time—had listened to Imperial Irishmen like T. W. Rolleston and had put into operation the plans for which they pleaded, what misery would have been avoided ! There were two main contentions running through every pronouncement, speech, article, or pamphlet made or written by my father on the subject of Ireland ; one was that if Irishmen were given something else to think about besides their grievances—legitimate or otherwise, but mostly the former—

[1] See pp. 46/47.

those grievances would be forgotten ; the other was that if England were to assist industrial development in Ireland on a far larger scale than Ireland could possibly manage by herself then Southern prosperity would soon begin to be commensurate with that of Ulster and, as a result, North and South must eventually come together naturally—drawn to each other under a common industrial banner.

Home Rule of course had been killed by the Easter Rising and its consequences, and, after brutally stupid attempts to rule Southern Ireland by force, the British Government in effect washed its hands of the whole business, gave Ulster to the Northern industrialists, threw the South to the wolves of ' Republicanism ', and sat back to draw ' annuities ' at the rate of four or five million a year in respect of land that never originally belonged to England at all. This arrangement was ratified in effect by the 1921 Treaty. What a policy of despair to put beside such a plan as that outlined in the interview of which the main points have just been quoted !

But it may not be too late. South and North have both marched for nearly twenty years in opposite directions, but they *can* be brought back to the cross-roads. Ulster of course will have to be left alone for the present, though she must be made to undertake not to interfere and in particular not to indulge in provocations such as her recent (February 1938) General Election. Then the South must be invited to become what she has never been except on paper—an actual part of the United Kingdom ; not a Dominion but a real part of the parent body of all Dominions, a position which connotes politically a far higher status. Then, with the annuities either cancelled,[1] heavily reduced, or re-spent in Ireland, a policy which will recognise that an Irish county shall be just as much part of the United Kingdom as Surrey or Yorkshire will soon create a good will in Ireland that almost every action of England for the last seven hundred years has crushed out of existence as soon as it has shown signs of birth.

Irish people—true sentimentalists—are responsive to decent treatment, but they can hate just as deeply as they can love, and anything like the raw deal to which they are accustomed will always bring their worst qualities to the surface. I do

---

[1] This has of course been done.

not wish to paint my fellow-countrymen as something like misunderstood angels, but Heaven knows they have had plenty of provocation. They have never, even after the reform of the Penal Laws and the granting of the right for Irish Roman Catholics to be educated, had equal treatment with English people ; vested interests in England and Scotland have operated to prevent proper use being made of the country and its potentialities—particularly of its harbours—and whenever an English politician has turned his thoughts to the country, he has seemed to do it in the manner of a parent regarding a spoilt child, forgetful of the fact that the child did not spoil itself.

I do not think any unprejudiced observer can regard Mr. de Valera's régime as having been much of a success. He and his Government, having spent their time being rude to England, have reached a point where the country finds itself in a well-nigh desperate situation. Farming is in a shocking state and every one who can do so is leaving the country. Soon there will be no one left to reap the benefit of the new state of affairs. The time is therefore ripe for a return to the cross-roads, but whatever England does must be done, not in the spirit of granting a concession but of recognising and conceding long-withheld rights. Southampton and the other big English and Scottish ports may throw their weight and influence and money into the scale in opposition to the opening up of a western harbour, and the Midlands may lobby against the development of Irish industry, but they must not be listened to ; they must be made to understand that Ireland is to be really in the Union and is not to be discriminated against any longer.

The 1938 ' Pact with Eire ' was a step in the right direction and if some such programme as above—or some step in that direction—should follow it we may look forward to a happier state of affairs and in the ' long run '—now perhaps a bit longer than it need have been—to a really united Ireland, because Ulster will eventually ask to be allowed to re-unite herself with the now mangled country to which she belongs.

My father said his penultimate word on the subject in his 1919 pamphlet, ' Ireland's Vanishing Opportunity '. This publication, while applauding Sinn Fein's success in eliminating the old political party, was in the main an urgent appeal to the party in power in the South to give up clamouring for a Home Rule that, without Ulster, would be the hollow mockery it has since proved to be, and to press for a real union with England—to demand in fact the conversion of the Act of Union into a reality and not a paper sham.

I am wholly with the Sinn Feiners in the conviction that we need a new policy for Ireland, but it must be a policy of sincerity and reality. I am convinced that Home Rule will in the end be thrust upon us whether we will or no. That cause was essentially won many years ago ; all we have to do is to try not to get in the way of it. But at the present moment it can only come in the guise of dismemberment, and against that we must be adamant. Nor should we accept any form of Home Rule which will lessen our due proportionate share of Parliamentary power. This means that Home Rule should be deferred in favour of a programme of more immediate urgency—a programme which in fact will prove to be the best possible preparation for self-government. We must join hands with Ulster in declaring for equality within the Union, and in compelling Parliament to do us justice, and to do it in the precise manner which we, after taking counsel together, shall prescribe. How much there is to understand and master in the condition of Ireland at the present day ! Education, Poor Law reform, the completion of Land Purchase, the development of co-operation, the establishment of rural credit, the examination and opening up of mineral resources, the securing of fair play for Irish manufacturers in the matter of public contracts, the co-ordination and development of the railway service and of waterways—and above all, and first of all, the grand project of linking Ireland with the two Continents to east and west —is this not a wide enough, a fair enough, field for patriotic toil ? All these things can be done without waiting for Home Rule. Under any form of Home Rule which is possible at present the most important of them would have to be renounced for ever ; we should have missed a tide which will never again be at flood upon the shores of Ireland. Ireland has never failed when she spoke with one voice in demanding objects of this kind. It was thus we got the Wyndham Act, and we would have it still had not the Parliamentary Party insisted on repealing it. It was thus we obtained the Department of Agriculture ; we have yet to discover what we cannot obtain in this way. And these are objects in which, perhaps with a little give and take on the education question, the whole of Ireland can unite. What might not come of that unity of thought and action over a great and varied field of Irish reform ? Ulster and the rest of Ireland are now like oil and water ; it is useless to try to mix them by shaking the bottle ; every time we set it down they part again inexorably. But when substances in chemistry will not combine we can often persuade them to do so by introducing some third element which has an apparently magical effect in overcoming their mutual repulsion. Let us try a little political alchemy in Ireland. If Ulster and the South can be caught up in a great national tide of economic development and social reform—if they come out together into the new world, the world of reality and progress, they will never part again ; what they do they will plan together and execute together ; we shall make Ireland one as she has never been in all her history. The thing can be done—it is crying to be done !

Four months before he died T. W. Rolleston's last word was written in an article in the *Nineteenth Century* of August 1920, which concluded :

' Every affair,' said Epictetus, ' has two handles ; by the one you can carry it, by the other you cannot.' The Irish problem has the political handle and what we may call, though the word does not quite sum up the idea, the economic handle. Every one who has tried to take hold of it by the political handle has burnt his own fingers and done more harm than good. Think of Gladstone, Rosebery, Birrell, Asquith, Lloyd George— did history ever teach a lesson in clearer terms ? But those who have grasped the economic handle—Drummond, Arthur Balfour, Gerald Balfour, Plunkett, Wyndham (before the two latter yielded to the fatal attraction of politics)—have prospered and made Ireland prosper ; they have been the reconciling and creative forces in recent Anglo-Irish history.

Politicians greedy for power, ignorant of history, or bemused with phrases, and commercial rings, jealous now as ever of Irish progress, have conspired with Irish folly and criminality to lay their noble work in the dust. To rebuild and complete it is the one thing needful. Parliament is trying at present to settle Ireland by forcing on it a measure which the whole country dreads and detests. Why not give, instead, something that the whole country will welcome—something already granted in name and form and only needing to be put into effective operation ? All the legislation that is needed was passed one hundred and twenty years ago. Nobody in Ireland wants Home Rule under any form at present practicable. But all Ireland, without any exception whatever, wants the Union —that is to say, so long as the forms of the Union and the taxation of the Union still subsist, it wants also the advantages of the Union ; it wants full and unreserved equality. And if, after this, any political resettlement proves still desirable, this is the shortest road to it ; political reform will come with ease and automatically once the true basis of imperial unity has been firmly and irrevocably laid. That basis lies in the establishment of an economic connection of such a character that Ireland shall feel her interests to be vitally linked with those of Great Britain. Anti-English feeling in Ireland, so far as it is not a mere transitory sentiment born of the madness and violence of the present hour, springs in reality from the sense that Ireland has been put by Nature into a corner, and that England has taken advantage of the circumstances to keep her there. She very properly wants to get out, and many Irishmen are under the delusion that the Sinn Fein programme could take her out. But that is just what it cannot do ; it would lock her up in her corner for ever ; for it would merely set Great Britain free to use all her powers to keep Ireland poor and dependent.

But these are possibilities which at present few Englishmen contemplate. The connection must remain—the problem is to make it honourable and profitable for both parties, and I submit that the way to this end is clear.

Clear, but not altogether easy, for it involves the defeat of the powerful commercial ring ; it involves making Liverpool and Manchester and Southampton understand that they must not decree for ever the empty desolation of the great havens of Western Ireland. Nevertheless, here, if anywhere, is the true lever by which this intolerable and shameful load of the Irish problem can be rolled from England. Shall we ever see a British statesman who will set his hand to it?

Nineteen years have passed since T. W. Rolleston died and Irish affairs have gone from bad to worse. The signs are not hopeful of any great step forward ; a Trade Treaty, we know, has been negotiated, but this savours of mere tinkering.

There is one ray of hope—a possibility that the British statesman for whom T. W. Rolleston was looking may be on the stage at this moment. The Secretary of State for Dominion Affairs, Mr. Malcolm MacDonald, is a Scot and a Celt and should be able to look at the Irish situation through un-blinkered eyes. Should he do that and should he grasp the ' handle ' by which the ' affair ' can be carried, the sun of prosperity and happiness may after all begin to rise over the Irish Sea.[1]

[1] This was written before the re-arrangement of Cabinet posts which took Mr. MacDonald away from the Dominions Office.

VII

VERSE

THE preceding portions of this book indicate I think that, even if he had had no interests or occupations other than those already mentioned, T. W. Rolleston must have led a very full and useful life. Many a man would be deemed to have done as much as could be expected of any one man in a lifetime if this brief account of my father's life and work had now to be brought to an end. But the facts are otherwise ; hitherto I have dealt almost exclusively with work my father did either to help other people or to further the interests of his country as he saw them ; it is time now to turn to a consideration of his activities in a more personal field—to work which he may be said in fact to have done for himself, for he was always under the necessity of earning an income.

I do not know when my father began to write verse ; the earliest record of note dates back to his time as an Undergraduate at Trinity College, Dublin, in about 1876, when he won the Vice-Chancellor's Prize for English Verse. His entry for this prize was called ' The Feast of Belshazzar ', but all trace of the poem itself has been lost. My stepmother's theory is that, in later years, Rolleston did not have any very high regard for what he had written and therefore purposely failed to keep a copy of it and did not include it in a little volume of verse and verse translations which was published in 1909 by Maunsel and Company of Dublin under the title *Sea Spray.*

At that time—when he was at T.C.D.—Rolleston, as has already been stated, became greatly attracted by Walt Whitman, and his translation, with S. K. Knortz, of *Leaves of Grass* into German appeared in 1880, when he was living in Germany. At the same period he was also contributing to *Kottabos*,[1] and the issue for Hilary Term, 1882, has as its opening item a

[1] See p. 96.

poem by ' T.W.R.' called ' Calvin Harlowe ', which tells the story of the last soldier in Fort Steadman during the American Civil War who preferred to die rather than surrender to the temporarily victorious Southern Army—

> Praise for the brave no duty bound
>   To waste their lives for valour's sake ;
> But who shall praise the dead who found
>   The words ' I yield ' too hard to speak ?

This poem was inspired by an episode related by Walt Whitman in his *Memoranda of the American Civil War* and, together with Rolleston's verses *From the German of Uhland*, quoted on page 96, provides a starting-point for a consideration of the whole of his writings in verse.

The theme that seems to run through all, or nearly all, of Rolleston's poetry may be expressed in one word—' Action '. He seldom wrote on ephemeral or intangible subjects such as clouds or flowers or imaginary goddesses ; he *did* write of men and women—real or legendary—who had done things, who had been men and women of action ; or he wrote of personal experiences or of things and places he had seen and which were perhaps shrines or monuments of men of deeds. Rolleston was himself essentially a man of action ; if he saw something that needed to be done he could not be content till he had done it or, if it were not within the range of his own abilities, till he had inspired some one else more suitable to undertake the task. No verse therefore reflects more accurately than his the thoughts and aspirations of the writer. Rolleston was always striving to achieve something and, like the truest type of workman, he gloried in looking back on something he knew he had done well. He cared little whether others praised it ; provided it satisfied him that was all he asked for, and the standards he set himself were higher perhaps than he would have set for others. It was quite natural therefore that his admiration for achievement should inspire so much of his verse ; and, if such achievement required vigour or tenacity in the face of difficulties, those qualities shone out in what he wrote.

One of my father's favourite forms of holiday when he was a young man took him up and down the Irish coast in a frail Rob Roy canoe, accompanied often by his great friend of those days, Jack Humphreys. To venture in a Rob Roy canoe on the waters of a placid lake would be for many people an adventure of considerable magnitude, but for T. W. R. placid lakes had no appeal ; there were no risks to face, no waves to surmount, nothing to overcome ; so his canoe, which he had built himself, spelt for him and his companion the open sea, and there are few bays or coves on the east coast of their native land into which their fragile craft did not nose their way.

'Sea Spray', the title poem in the little book already mentioned, commemorates those days ; in its vivid lines it is easy to detect that my father's love of the sea and of the vigour it demands from those who would venture into close contact with it was tempered with the true sailor's respect for its angrier moods :

> What shall we do with our day ? You ask—
>   A June day fair to the heart's desire—
> Lie in the meadow, and lounge and bask
>   Over books and tobacco ? Or do you aspire
> To conquer the summit that yesterday
>   We marked for our own ere your visit end ?
> Or shall we go riding, or fishing ? Nay,
>   For the scent of the sea's on the air, my friend.
> We shall go to the head of the reedy lake,
>   And there, in a brake by a fir grove find
> Two long canoes with arching deck,
>   Sea-riders, strong for a day of wind ;
> And oh, what a song shall the bright wind sing us,
>   When clear of the shallows and clear of the sedge,
> While the narrowing stream and the ebb-tide swing us
>   'Twixt sea and mountain to Wicklow Bridge !

> But here beware ! For the ebb goes roaring
>   Through half the arches, and half are dry,
> And stakes and stones are ready for goring
>   Your Rob Roy's timbers as down you fly.
> And beyond the Bridge, in the deep sea-current,
>   Where the rope-maze crosses from quay to quay,
> You'll need your head and your arm I warrant,
>   To fight the eddies and find your way.
> There lifts your prow with the long pulsation
>   That tells how near us the glad seas are !
> There lifts the heart with the old elation,
>   To meet the surf at the harbour-bar !

The North wind marshals the ranks of ocean,
  And on they sweep with a strength serene,
Till the tide-race ruffles the mighty motion
  And curls the crests of the rollers green.
The breakers flash on the sand-bank yonder,
  And the cavern'd curve of the rock-walled bay
Is loud with clamour of hoarse sea-thunder
  As the wave recoils in a blast of spray.

And I know a cleft among grim rock-masses,
  Where if wind blow strong and the light come fair,
When the sea-cave roars and the spray-jet flashes,
  A rainbow floats in the sunny air.

At the Head's wild verge, where the tideways quicken,
  And eddies hollow the smooth sea-caves,
Our Rob Roys plunge as the breakers thicken,
  And bury their decks in the rearing waves.
We round the point in the surge and welter
  Of clashing billows and blinding foam—
Then mile on mile, in the cliff-wall's shelter,
  In calm new seas to the South we roam.

O bays of Wicklow, and gorse-crowned headlands
  Whose scent blows far on the seaward breeze,
How oft have I yearned in the tranquil midlands
  For one brave shock of your lifting seas !
How oft it may be in the days hereafter
  Shall rise the thought of you, phantom-fair,
Shall steal the sound of the sea-waves' laughter
  On ears grown dull with time and care !
Waves, wash my spirit, and lonely places,
  If well I loved you, and aught you knew,
Mark deep my heart with immortal traces
  Of shining days when I dwelt with you !

T. W. Rolleston did a good deal of translation into English
verse from the Greek, Latin, and German, and the following
passage from Aeschylus' account of the Battle of Salamis as
related by the messenger sent by Xerxes to tell his mother,
Atossa, of his defeat is another excellent example of the appeal
made to my father by a story full of incident, movement,
exertion, and energy. I cannot reproduce the whole poem,
but the following is part of the messenger's story which surely
conjures up a picture as vivid as any words could make it :

Then the heart-kindling trumpet spake, and then
We heard the thunder of a thousand oars
That swung together at the steersman's cry,
And all at once the sounding furrows smote.
Then soon full clear their charging line we saw,
The right wing leading, and the main array
A little after ; and ere long we heard
Such cries as these : ' On, children of the Greek !
Now for your fatherland, for freedom now !
For wife and child, and for your fathers' homes !
Now for the temples of your fathers' gods,
To-day we fight for all ! ' So cried they still,
Nor were we Persians dumb, but sent them back
Shouting for shouting. Little time there was
To range our lines, until the brazen beaks
Crash'd in among us.

It would not be proper for me to say that my father was
a great poet in the absence of any general expression of contemporary opinion to that effect ; nor would he himself
have dreamed of making such a claim. Yet his poetry deserves
to be much better known ; it is all so direct, so unambiguous,
so easy to read and comprehend, so different from much that
has usurped the word ' poetry ' to-day ; he never used words
for the sake of any mere beauty of rhythm they might possess
or because the words themselves conveyed in pleasing sounds
some thought not strictly appropriate to the subject about
which he might be writing. Every line and every word of
Rolleston's verse had a meaning and was included because
of that meaning and for no other reason at all. If the poem
was to tell a story it went straightly on with the tale and
never wandered off into side-tracks or strained to conjure up
fanciful similes. Take this narrative of ' The Flight of O'Donnell ' from *Poems and Ballads of Young Ireland* ; it begins with
a prose introduction :

A.D. 1590. It is related that Hugh Roe O'Donnell, who had been
three years a prisoner of the English, effected his escape from Dublin
Castle, towards the close of the winter of 1589–90. He made his way
over the Three Rock Mountain (Slieve Roe) to the neighbourhood of
Powerscourt, where was the Castle of Phelim O'Toole, a cousin of Barnaby
O'Toole, of Castlekevin. Here O'Donnell found himself unable from
fatigue to walk any further—his shoes too had been torn from his feet
in the rough and wet way he had passed ; so he applied for succour to
O'Toole, who had visited him in prison, and whom, although an ally of
the English, he had reason to think his friend.

From Dublin Castle by bleak Slieve Roe
  He has toiled o'er bog and stone,
And the streaming rain and the winter wind
  Have chilled him to the bone.

He has toiled through all the winter night,
  And now at last he hears
The Dargle's voice in the Wicklow Hills
  Sing liberty in his ears.

For Phelim O'Toole has his Castle there,
  An Irish heart and hearth ;
And thither for shelter and succour turns
  The young eagle of the North.

' God knows, O'Donnell ', the chieftain cried,
  ' A sorrowful man you see.
If Fitzwilliam were ware that you sheltered here
  I should hang from my own roof-tree.'

O'Donnell arose with never a word
  And strode to the open door,
And every print of his naked feet
  Was blood upon Phelim's floor.

' Now hold, O'Donnell ', cried Phelim's wife,
  ' May bard ne'er tell the tale
That O'Toole drove out to his English foe
  The hope of the whole Clan Gael.

' But mark me, husband, the rede I give :
  Bid saddle a slow-foot mule—
To bear word to the Council, O'Donnell Oge
  Is the prisoner of O'Toole.

' But first the pick of thy stables choose
  A steed both swift and sure,
And give thy stoutest rider word
  To gallop to Glenmalure.

' MacHugh O'Bryne will ride full sharp
  At Tanist O'Donnell's call,
And or ever the Deputy's men win home
  Right many a thing may fall.'

'Tis the stoutest rider by Dargle side,
  On a steed both swift and sure ;
And he spurs amain through the blinding rain
  To the Valley of Glenmalure.

' Rise up, MacHugh ! There's a prey for you
  The like you never drove ;
Red Hugh O'Donnell in Phelim's hall
  Begs help for his country's love.

' Rise up and ride, for this rain of doom
   Is melting the solid earth ;
And the Annamoe and the Glenmacnass
   They foamed at my horse's girth.'

MacHugh bade saddle, and rode full fast
   Adown the wondrous Vale,
And forty horsemen spurred hard behind
   The terror of all the Pale.

At Laragh they forded the Glenmacnass
   And marvelled such flood to see,
And the yellow tide that was Annamoe
   Splashed many a rider's knee.

By the bogs of Togher, the slopes of Djouce,
   They rode with toil and pain,
Till they heard the Falls in their dread ravine
   Roar far through the clouds of rain.

But fierce the tawny river ran
   'Neath the Castle of O'Toole,
Till it thundered down in a sunless gorge,
   From seething pool to pool.

MacHugh he gazed on the foaming ford,
   And an angry man was he,
And thrice he drove his stumbling steed
   Breast-high in that raging sea.

And thrice the midstream's outer whirl
   Had all but swept him down :
' I doubt I were paid for this ', he said,
   ' With the burning of Dublin town.

' I had rather Hugh were in Glenmalure
   Than the plunder of all the Pale ;
And the Deputy's men in the Dargle flood,
   And Phelim O'Toole in hell '.

MacHugh rides back to Glenmalure
   With a sorrowful pace and slow,
And O'Donnell rides fast into Dublin town
   In the hand of his deadly foe.

Yet take heart, Red Hugh ! Not this the end,
   Thy day is still to come ;
And the clansmen's shout and the sworded hand
   And the stately northern home.

ENTRANCE TO GLENMALURE

JOHN O'LEARY, 1894

> Take heart, Red Hugh ! There is work to do,
> The land hath need of thee ;
> For a heart of fire to swell her veins
> From farthest sea to sea
> With the pulse of power and the pride of strife
> And the rapture of victory.

I have incorporated in this one or two minor amendments made by my father in the copy of the *Poems and Ballads* that he gave my mother after publication.

The story of Ireland inspired a good deal of Rolleston's earlier verse, though not so much as might have been expected from a man who was so deeply affected by his country's misfortunes. This is probably accounted for by his four years of residence in Germany from 1879 to 1883, when the spell of Heine, Goethe, and Lessing added other non-Irish influences to the effect already produced on him by Walt Whitman. However, the *Poems and Ballads of Young Ireland* is one of the early sign-posts on the road to the Irish Literary Revival and the place of honour in it was given to my father's dedication of the book to John O'Leary, the great and lovable old Fenian leader. I remember O'Leary well, with his wild shaggy appearance and long white beard. My sister, Una, was devoted to him ; she would sit on his knee and listen to his stories for hours on end and be perfectly happy. For John O'Leary, for all that he was the leader of a rebellion and had been transported for seven years, was gentle and kind.

> Because you suffered for the cause ;
> Because you strove with voice and pen
> To serve the Law above the laws
> That purifies the hearts of men ;
>
> Because you failed, and grew not slack,
> Nor sullen, nor disconsolate ;
> Nor stooped to seek a lower track,
> But showed your soul a match for fate ;
>
> Because you hated all things base,
> And held your country's honour high ;
> Because you wrought in time and space
> Not heedless of Eternity ;
>
> Because you loved the nobler part
> Of Erin ; so we bring you here
> Words such as once the nation's heart
> On patriot lips rejoiced to hear :

Strains that have little chance to live
  With those that Davis' clarion blew,
But all the best we have to give,
  To mother Erin and to you.

In a different vein is ' Ceres ' written while Rolleston was
either at school or at Trinity, probably between 1871 and
1877 and certainly before 1879, the year of his first marriage,
for it exists only in manuscript, together with three other sets
of verses which were given to my mother while she was still
Edith de Burgh.

Thou art lost to the land of the living,
  My daughter, and vainly I weep,
For our joys and our loves and our grieving
  Are lighter than visions of sleep ;
Yet I wander with ceaseless complaining
  The fields that Proserpina trod,
Though I know that my daughter is reigning
    The bride of a God.

And pale as the spirits before her
  She harks to their groaning and sighs,
And Tartarus bends to adore her,
  Who rules with implacable eyes ;
For the nether-God took her and throned her,
  When the flowers of her girlhood were shed,
And all the wide universe owned her,
    The Queen of the dead.

The Pomegranate hardened for ever
  The lips that were sweet upon earth ;
They are beautiful still, but with never
  A savour of mourning or mirth ;
But calm and unaltered she gazes
  With languid, inflexible eyes
On the horror of desolate places
  Where woe never dies.

But I am bereaved of a daughter
  Though Hell be possessed of a Queen.
O meadows of Enna, with slaughter
  Defiled be the pride of your green,
And faded the flowers that won her
  To wander a perilous way,
Where the God as an eagle upon her
  Swept down on his prey.

There is a rather macabre echo of Swinburne about ' Ceres '
which, one is glad to notice, disappeared from my father's

later work, enabling him to write of death and the dead in the far more heroic and inspiring strain of ' The Dead at Clonmacnois '. This grand poem is included in many anthologies, including *The Oxford Book of English Verse*, and is a translation from the Irish of Angus O'Gillan. Clonmacnois, on the bank of the Shannon in King's County, was the burial place of the ancient Kings of Ireland—a spot as sacred to Irish people as the Holy Hill of Tara itself :

> In a quiet watered land, a land of roses,
>   Stands Saint Kieran's city fair ;
> And the warriors of Erin in their famous generations
>   Slumber there.
>
> There beneath the dewy hillside sleep the noblest
>   Of the Clan of Conn,
> Each below his stone with name in branching Ogham
>   And the sacred knot thereon.
>
> There they laid to rest the seven Kings of Tara,
>   There the sons of Cairbré sleep—
> Battle-banners of the Gael, that in Kieran's plain of crosses
>   Now their final hosting keep.
>
> And in Clonmacnois they laid the men of Teffia,
>   And right many a lord of Breagh ;
> Deep the sod above Clan Creide and Clan Conaill,
>   Kind in hall and fierce in fray.
>
> Many and many a son of Conn the Hundred-Fighter
>   In the red earth lies at rest ;
> Many a blue eye of Clan Colman the turf covers,
>   Many a swan-white breast.

These lovely lines first appeared in *Poems and Ballads of Young Ireland* in 1888, and were reprinted in *A Treasury of Irish Poetry* in 1900, and in *Sea Spray* in 1909.

T. W. Rolleston was also well represented in *Dublin Verses by Members of Trinity College*, edited by H. A. Hinkson and published in 1895 by Elkin Mathews of London and Hodges, Figgis, and Co., Ltd. of Dublin. My father's contributions to that collection were five in number and included a delicious morsel for which my sister, Una, was responsible. When Una was about five or six years of age she complained that she could not understand father's poems because the words were too long ; she asked for a poem for herself and ' For a Reading Lesson ' was the result :

> ' Papa, did you make that song ? '
>   Said my Una : ' Much too long
> Are those words for me to spell.
>   Make a little song as well,
> Full of little words for me,
>   " To " and " by " and " of " and " the "—
> " Mama " must be in it too—
>   Then I'll read it all for you.'

> ' Una, if that song were made
>   As you bid me ', Papa said,
> ' Full of love and little words,
>   Who would listen to the birds ?
> Could I make it right for you,
>   All the world would read it too '.

In 1891 and 1892 T. W. Rolleston was living in London and, with Ernest Rhys and W. B. Yeats, founded the famous Rhymers' Club. This association of youngish poets met regularly over a period of about two years at the Cheshire Cheese which was, and still is, in Wine Office Court off Fleet Street. Here the company would first perhaps dine and afterwards smoke long churchwarden pipes, drink beer, and read to each other their latest verses. In the first year of the Club's existence there were only twelve actual members, but many ' associates '. The twelve were Ernest Dowson, Edwin J. Ellis, G. A. Greene, Lionel Johnson, Richard Le Gallienne, Victor Plarr, Ernest Radford, Ernest Rhys, T. W. Rolleston, Arthur Symons, John Todhunter, and W. B. Yeats. Later the number became thirteen by the addition of Arthur Cecil Hillier.

The Rhymers' Club published two small volumes in 1892 and 1894—*The Book of the Rhymers' Club* and *The Second Book of the Rhymers' Club*, to both of which Rolleston of course contributed. In the first book he well caught the spirit of the Club and the atmosphere of the old Tavern in which the members met, with his ' Ballade of the Cheshire Cheese ' :

> I know a home of antique ease
>   Within the smoky city's pale,
> A spot wherein the spirit sees
>   Old London through a thinner veil.

The modern world, so stiff and stale,
　You leave behind you, when you please,
For long clay pipes and great old ale
　And beefsteaks in the Cheshire Cheese.

Beneath this board Burke's, Goldsmith's knees
　Were often thrust—so runs the tale—
'Twas here the Doctor took his ease,
　And wielded speech that, like a flail,
Threshed out the golden truth : All hail
　Great souls ! that met on nights like these,
Till morning made the candles pale,
　And revellers left the Cheshire Cheese.

By kindly sense, and old decrees
　Of England's use, they set their sail—
We press to never-furrowed seas,
　For vision-worlds we breast the gale,
And still we seek and still we fail,
　For still the ' glorious phantom ' flees—
Ah, well ! No phantoms are the ale
　And beefsteaks of the Cheshire Cheese.

Envoi

If doubts or debts thy soul assail,
　If Fashion's forms its current freeze,
Try a long pipe, a glass of ale,
　And supper at the Cheshire Cheese.

In *The Second Book of the Rhymers' Club* Rolleston published
' Morning : A Cycling Song ', ' Noon-day (Elegiacs) ', and
' Night : After All '. The first of these acts as a reminder
that my father was an ardent cyclist ; he thought—and
rightly—that there was no more satisfactory way of seeing a
country while at the same time supplying one's lungs with
fresh air and one's muscles with exercise than to go for a bicycle
tour. He must have penetrated on his machine to almost
every corner of Ireland, besides going for many extended
tours in Germany, Switzerland, and England. Originally he
rode one of the old high bicycles, sometimes called ' Penny-
farthings ', though more usually known in those days as
' Giraffes '. Douglas Hyde tells the story of how one day,
wanting to go to Lucan near Dublin, Rolleston offered to
lend him his Giraffe for the purpose. ' When,' writes Hyde,
' I said I was afraid to ride anything so high lest it might
skid and the bike be injured, Rolleston said he was not thinking
of that at all but of the future of Irish literature '.

'Morning' was a tribute to his bicycle; the last verse and refrain went:

> Oh, there's many a one who teaches that the shining river reaches
> Are the place to spend a long June day;
> But give me the whirling wheel and a boat of air and steel
> To float upon the Queen's highway!
>
> Oh, give me the kiss of the morning breeze,
> And the rose of the morning sky,
> And the long brown road where the tired spirit's load
> Slips off as the leagues go by.

Rossall School adopted 'Morning' as a school song with music by E. T. Sweeting, Mus. Bac., F.C.O., but gave it an awful title—'My Pneumatic'!

As I have said, the Rhymers' Club had a comparatively short life and, on its dissolution, one member at least completely lost touch with his erstwhile colleagues. That was Richard Le Gallienne, who, many years afterwards while lecturing in America, told the story of the Club, concluding with the information that all the other members had either died of drink or gone mad! I remember my father's amusement when he read in an American paper of the untimely end to which he had come; a more sane or sober person than T. W. Rolleston it would be hard to imagine, but his sense of humour, always very near the surface, prevented him from being the least bit annoyed.

In Donegal on one occasion this same sense of humour found an opportunity to manifest itself at the expense of the Royal and Ancient game of golf. My father's cycling tours on business or for pleasure often took him to Ireland's north-western county, whose cliffs and bays, sandy beaches and rocky off-shore islands provide the world with some of its grandest scenery. Rolleston was not a golfer and the Rosapenna Hotel on the shores of Mulroy Bay, where he often stayed, was normally full of golfers drawn thither by the excellent links. Conversation was therefore almost entirely confined to golf and golf stories, but, though the game still draws hundreds to Rosapenna, few of to-day's visitors probably know of the famous match that was played there in the imagination of T. W. Rolleston. It seems he must have tired of being unable to partake of the standard conversational fare, so he decided to poke a little fun at the ancient game—

so ancient in fact that even Cuchullin seems to have known of it, though it will be noticed that in this account, taken from *Kottabos* of 1894, of his match with Fingall, the contestants did not succeed in playing any golf :

A Legend of the North.
Gleaned on the shores of Mulroy Bay.

Long ago, in old, ancient times, there lived an Irish giant named Cuchullin and a Scottish giant named Fingall. Both of these had met with, and had conquered in every variety of warlike and manly exercise, every champion in their respective countries ; and having now nothing left to achieve, they spent their time in recounting their past exploits, and others which they would have performed had the opportunity been granted to them. And this at last became very grievous, for the giants were naturally able to compel the attention of whomsoever they would, nor would they tolerate any other subject of conversation. And to put an end to this affliction nothing seemed better to their friends and kinsfolk than to bring about a contest between these two heretofore invincible heroes. Accordingly, when Fingall, who had all his life addicted himself with great fervour to the game of golf, was next heard to boast of his triumphs in that pastime, he was asked why he so long delayed to set the crown on his achievements by defeating the mighty Cuchullin, who, they said, had recently declared himself to be without a rival in the mystery and science of that ancient and royal game. Thereupon Fingall grew full of wrath and vowed that he would silence for ever that lying and boasting tongue, were it not that it stood not with his dignity to enter upon a contest with a baby and a weakling, ' For ', he said, ' it is but twenty years since Cuchullin first began to learn the game of golf. Nevertheless ', he added, ' no man shall say that I ever shrank from any encounter ; and if Cuchullin will but prove that he is able to swing my clubs, I will play with him when and where he will.' And word of this was brought to Cuchullin. And when they told him that before Fingall would meet him he must first prove that he was able to swing Fingall's clubs, he laughed, and said, ' That will be an easy matter for me. But tell Fingall that before *I* meet *him* he must prove to me that he is able to lift my ball ; and if he abide this test, I will play him when and where he will.' And Fingall agreed to this, and began to practise with a boulder of three tons weight.

And the Champions met, with a great concourse of friends and followers and kinsfolk, at Rosapenna Hotel, where are known to be the noblest golf links in the world. And they surveyed each other, and each was struck with the other's majesty and strength and manly grace, yet each smiled with the assurance of coming victory. Then Fingall first threw down his bag of clubs upon the floor, and Cuchullin laid hold upon a niblick and endeavoured to draw it out. And as he tugged, the windows of Rosapenna Hotel rattled, but the niblick did not stir. And a second time he tugged with all his might, and the walls shook, but he could not draw it out. And then he set his teeth, and the veins in his forehead swelled, and he bowed his back and laid hold of the niblick, and the knuckles of his hands grew white. And as he tugged and strained the walls rocked, and the doors swung to and fro, and several of Welch's Irish Views fell from the walls. And outside the waves boiled upon the beach, and the seafowl wailed and clamoured, and a whirlwind arose, darkening all the air with flying sand. But the niblick never stirred by a hair's breadth, and Cuchullin sat down, saying he feared to do some damage ; at least the bystanders heard him mutter something that sounded rather like ' damage ', and they supposed that must have been what he meant.

Then when he was recovered, he rose up and went out to the Links, and Fingall with him, and he laid the ball upon the ground. Fingall approached it, and, fixing his eyes steadily upon it, he prepared to strike. But as he gazed, suddenly the ball disappeared from view, and a mist arose and swam before his eyes, and he staggered to and fro, and knew no longer where he was. Then, as he groped and cried out in alarm, the mist disappeared, and he again saw the ball, as before, resting upon the tee. And again he drew near, and fixed his eyes steadfastly upon the ball, and swung his club on high ; but again the mist enveloped him, and he could see the ball no more, and he heard the laughter of the spectators as they saw him grope and beat the air. Then a fear descended upon him such as he had never known, and he threw down the club, and vowed to attempt the feat no more, ' lest ', he said, ' I lose my senses and become unable to discern reality from falsehood any longer.'

Then Cuchullin said, ' We are both vanquished, O Fingall ; tell me now how it was that I could not draw out the niblick '. And Fingall said, ' It was small wonder that you could not, O Cuchullin, for I put an enchantment upon you, and that which you took for a niblick was Yggdrasil, the Ash Tree of the World, whose boughs are continents and its leaves are islands, and the birds in its branches are the leviathans and monsters of the deep, and its stem is the Axle-tree of the Earth. But what ', he asked, ' was the ball that I could not see ? '—' It was small wonder that you could not see it ', said Cuchullin, ' for I put an enchantment upon you, O Fingall, and the ball that disappeared from view whenever you looked closely at it was the Meaning of a Speech of Lord Rosebery.'

Then the followers of Fingall cheered and shouted for Fingall, and those of Cuchullin for Cuchullin ; but Fingall praised and magnified the fame and mighty deeds of Cuchullin, and Cuchullin those of Fingall. And they drank all that was in that bar. And neither of them boasted at all for full seven days ; nor did they ever boast again, or magnify their glory and their mighty deeds, beyond what is natural and necessary for a giant, and possible for common humanity to endure.

One of T. W. Rolleston's most signal services to the Irish Literary Revival was rendered during the last eighteen months of the nineteenth century. He had felt for some time that much of the poetry that was being written by the Revivalists and that had been written by their predecessors was in danger of being lost and that it should therefore be collected into one volume. Such writings had up to then appeared in various periodicals, many of them somewhat obscure, and occasionally in small volumes such as the *Poems and Ballads of Young Ireland, Dublin Verses*, and the Books of the Rhymers' Club, whose editions were small and not easily accessible. Rolleston therefore set himself to the task of rescuing this poetry—or at least a representative selection of it—from possible oblivion by editing a comprehensive anthology in which the reader would find everything in Anglo-Irish verse worthy of preservation. He secured the co-operation of his father-in-law, Stopford Brooke, who contributed by way of introduction a brief history of Irish poetry in the nineteenth century and wrote also an introductory notice to the works of Thomas Moore which the book contained.

Most of the other introductory notices were compiled by Rolleston himself, though help in this direction was freely given by W. B. Yeats, George Sigerson, D. J. O'Donoghue, George Russell, and others. Extensive biographical notices were also included with the result that when this anthology was published by Smith, Elder, and Company in 1900 it fully merited its title—*A Treasury of Irish Poetry in the English Tongue*.

In all one hundred and two authors were represented by three hundred and fifteen poems ranging from anonymous street ballads and 'rebel' songs like the *Shan van Vocht* to some of the loveliest works of the writers of the eighties and nineties.

The compilation of this book involved a great deal of painstaking labour and a vast amount of correspondence, but it was overwhelmingly well worth doing and, as with everything to which T. W. Rolleston set his hand and brain and heart, when he parted with the last corrected proof, he did so with the knowledge that yet another stone in the Irish Literary edifice had been well and firmly laid. Stopford Brooke concluded his introduction with these words :

The river of Irish poetry in the English language is yet in its youth. It rose a hundred years ago in the far-off hills, and wrought its turbulent way down the channelled gorge it carved for its stream out of its own mountains. Other streams have joined it, bearing with them various waters ; and it has only just now issued from the hills, and begun to flow in quieter and lovelier lands, glancing from ripple to pool and from pool to ripple, among woods and meadows, happy, and making its lovers happy. It is the youngest child of the Goddess Poesy. Let it be judged as a youth. In time, if it remain true to its country's spirit, the stream that has just emerged from the mountain torrent will become a noble river.

Between 1900 and 1909 Rolleston wrote practically no verse. For the first five of those years his time was fully taken up by his work for the Department of Agriculture and during the remainder of the period he was engaged, to the exclusion of almost everything else, in writing *Parallel Paths : A Study of Biology, Ethics, and Art,* to which further reference will be made.

It was not till after he had settled in London that he returned to poetry and set to work to re-tell the ancient stories of Tannhäuser, Lohengrin, and Parsifal in English verse, and to complete the quartet with ' The Ring of the Nibelung,' which was done in prose. In undertaking these difficult tasks my father's ability in the handling of verse-narrative found ample scope and I personally doubt if any subject treated in this manner has presented its story more vividly or in a way adhering more closely to the task of telling its tale in simple language shorn of all irrelevancies. This too was done with a dignity and grandeur that have seldom if ever been equalled ; listen for example to this passage telling of Tannhäuser's arrival at the Venusberg and his first meeting with Venus herself :

> Within a bower he stood, whose walls were hung
> With rose-red silk, and perfumed like the rose.
> No door there was, nor window, yet a light
> Filled it, that seemed to throb from her who sate
> Upon a golden throne and gazed at him.
> Aye, there she sate, the wonder of all worlds !
> Her red-gold hair flowed down on either side
> And curled about her feet. One ivory breast
> Was bare, and through the saffron robe she wore
> Her whiteness shone. Distraught and dumb he gazed,
> Till on her scarlet lips began to dawn
> A smile—how infinitely faint ! And then
> Even as a drift of snow on some high Alp,
> Sun-kissed, descends in thunder to the plain,
> So at her feet he broke and fell ; a cry
> Burst from her lips, his burning forehead dropped
> Upon her knees ; and soon within his hair
> He felt soft hands that trembled, and he felt
> Her odorous warmth bend over him ; he heard
> A voice that murmured like a bird that sings,
> Embowered deep in forest-leaves. It said :
> ' Tannhäuser—minstrel—warrior—and my Love,
> I have sought thee many days . . .' The sweet voice broke,
> And bathed in tears he lifted up his face
> To meet a kiss that turned his blood to flame ;
> And in a mist of fire his spirit swooned.

And this from ' Lohengrin ', the lines in which Elsa demands to know her husband's name and which describes the slaying of Count Telramund after he and the would-be assassins have broken into the bridal chamber :

' Oh, never, Elsa ', the Swan Knight spake,
' Shall we be sundered until thou break
The ban that lies on thee and me.'
But Elsa cried : ' How bitterly
Have I rued the pledge that I gave to thee——

' Never to know my husband's name,
As though the word were a badge of shame ;
Never to know of what kin thou art,
In the years gone by to have no part,
Nor in one closed corner within thy heart ! '

Pale, pale, he stood for a moment there,
In his eyes the dawn of a deadly fear.
' Elsa ', he cried, ' I charge thee stay,
Or ever the word of doom thou say,
The fatal word that I must obey ! '

But Elsa laughed, and half distraught
Her lover to her breast she caught.
' This shape of flesh I can make mine own,
Yea, mine for ever and mine alone,
But the spirit roams in a world unknown.

' What Powers soe're that dare decree
I shall not know my love as he knows me,
I brave and defy them ! Declare thy race,
Thy noble name and thy dwelling place,
And the issue be it in God's good grace ! '

Stark and aghast for a moment there
He gazed upon her in dumb despair,
When they heard the tramp of a hurrying throng
That stormed those echoing halls along
That had echoed last to the bridal song.

A shout, a crash, and the carven door
Lay shivered along the chamber floor,
And there stood Telramund, sword in hand,
And behind him many a battle-brand
And the tossing plumes of an arméd band.

But swift as a hawk hath Elsa flown
To the couch whereon the sword was thrown—
She hath thrust the hilt to the hand of her Knight,
And the blade sang clear as it leaped to light,
And the chamber rang with the roar of fight.

Then guards and knights came trampling in,
Till the King's voice thundered above the din,
And the weapons sank at the word he said ;
And the brightest blade was bathed in red,
And on the rushes the Count lay dead.

'Parsifal,' which came next, presented, by reason of the greater variety of incident in the story, a far more difficult task ; but it was triumphantly accomplished and throughout the six sections of the work it maintained to the full the promise of its opening lines, which told of the ' Coming of the Grail ' in response to Titurel's prayer for help against the pagan ravishers of Anjou :

A little while, O you who con this rhyme,
Stand at my side and watch the mists of Time
Part for a little while, and give to view
The red roofs of a town in old Anjou,
That cluster round a lofty rock and steep,
Whereon with broad blind walls and frowning keep
An ancient fortress towers. Here once did reign
The good King Titurel, with his sons twain,
The first named Gamuret, whose lust of fight
Was never stilled ; the next Anfortas hight,
Of whom are wondrous tidings still to say.

    The tale I tell is of ancient day,
Ere yet the sword of Charlemagne set free
From lawless strife and heathen savegery
That good land, mother of great kings to come.
But lately from the dying hand of Rome
Had fallen the Empire of the West : so poured
From North, from South, a countless heathen horde,
Raging for blood and spoil, and overthrew
Many a high throne, and many a prince they slew,
Wasting the land ; and here alone the might
Of Titurel, the valiant pious knight,
Still held them off, though sore bestead was he ;
And round his walls they eddied sullenly.

    On the high tower that still his banner bore
Behold the King alone ! The day is o'er—
Of all the changing year that holiest day,
When erst upon the Hill of Golgotha
He hung upon the Cross, whose shame and death
Filled with great glory and immortal breath
The common clay of man. Above the King
His blazoned banner on the winds of spring

Lifted and sank ; nor did those breezes bear
Sweet odours of the spring-time to him there,
But bitter smoke from many a smouldering brand.
So Titurel gazed across the ravaged land,
And thought upon his troop encamped below,
Faithful to death, but sorely wasted now,—
The one slight shield that warded yet from harm
That little world of tower and town and farm.
Then lifting to the stars a face that ne'er
He showed, except to Heaven—so like despair
Was the wild look upon his tortured brow ;
' O God ', he whispered, ' We are lost, if Thou
Send us no help in this extremity ;
For past all hope of human aid are we.
Thy will be done ; Thy cup of mortal pain
Shall we who bear Thy sign refuse to drain ?
But weak are we—scarce one unwounded knight
Followed my pennon from the last great fight.
Lord, if Thou send no succour we must die ! '

Deep silence fell ; the winds were hushed ; the sky
Laughed with innumerable lights ; and awe
Crept about Titurel's heart, for now he saw
One trembling Star begin to move and grow,
Expanding to a misty globe, that slow
Descending, near and nearer, seemed to move
To swelling music, till the vault above
Rang, all one rapturous cry. At last it dwelt
On the stone parapet, whereby he knelt
Dumb with amazement and a wild suspense ;
And then a flood of perfume struck his sense,
More sweet, him seemed, than ever did beguile
The wanderer sailing by an Indian isle,
As from their throbbing heart of silver light,
The wreathing mists dissolved, and gave to sight
A cup of crystal, great and smooth and fair,
Radiant amid the dusk it rested there ;
And as he stared on it, in rosy flame
About its rim the shapes of letters came
And vanished ; but he read them as they glowed :
' I am that Grail which held the Blood that flowed
For man's redemption on the bitter Tree ;
And where I am are strength and victory.'

These three lovely narratives were not by any means based
entirely on the operas of Richard Wagner, though my father
acknowledged a debt to those works. Actually, however, he
had gone back to the same early sources as Wagner had
consulted and indeed wrote of the last of the three : ' In the

tale of Parsifal the writer must admit that he has not found himself wholly in sympathy with this creation of Wagner's later thought. The story as here told is not a reproduction of the Wagnerian music-drama. It is rather, with certain borrowings from Wagner, a free rendering of the tale as it was told in the noblest of the medieval versions '. In this case Rolleston founded his re-telling of the story mainly on the long epic tale of Wolfram von Eschenbach, written in about the year 1200.

' Lohengrin ' adheres more closely to Wagner, chiefly, as my father explained, because ' the text is so intimately associated with the music and has so little independent form of its own that " Lohengrin " seemed to require different treatment. . . . In general the shape given by Wagner to the story has been adhered to, but a new turn has been given to the episode of the fatal question and the broken pledge. Lohengrin and Elsa are drawn as having been both of them in the right.'

' Tannhäuser ' followed Wagner still more closely, the work, the first of the three to be published, being ' simply presented as being, as nearly as possible, Wagner's drama in narrative form '.

These three books were beautifully illustrated by Willy Pogány, the then almost unknown but afterwards celebrated Hungarian artist, and at least one copy of ' Parsifal ' achieved a certain fame. This copy, in a special binding bearing in its centre, on the outside cover, a small crystal reproduction of the Holy Grail, was given as a wedding present to Princess Patricia of Connaught. The cost of the binding and of the cutting of the crystal came to eighty guineas and the book was placed on view for several days in the window of J. and E. Bumpus' bookshop when that establishment was still on the north side of Oxford Street.

' Tannhäuser ', ' Lohengrin ', and ' Parsifal ' were published by George G. Harrap and Company in 1911, 1912, and 1913 and the following year should have seen the fourth of the quartet, ' The Ring of the Nibelung ', on the market. Rolleston completed it but, when the war broke out, it became of course impossible to issue any book having the remotest German flavour. Further to that Willy Pogány, as a Hungarian and therefore technically an alien enemy, went to

America where he has since devoted his great talents to other art forms with conspicuous success, notably in the world of the theatre. That, at any rate, is Mr. Harrap's account of the loss of Pogány as illustrator of ' The Ring ' given in his book of reminiscences, *Some Memories : 1901 to 1935*, but I find another explanation in my father's diary where, on 25 February 1914—long before the war was thought of—he wrote :

> I lunched with Harrap and his partner, Anderson, to-day. He told me relations between him and Pogány had been strained of late over the ' Nibelungen Ring '—and that he had decided not to bring it out this year, and probably P. would not illustrate it. I strongly urged E. J. Sullivan.

So ' The Ring ' has never been published and I am greatly obliged to the late Mr. George Harrap, owner of all four copyrights, for lending me his typescript and for giving permission to quote from it within reason. ' The Ring ', was written in four parts, ' The Rhinegold ', ' The Valkyrie ', ' Siegfried ', and ' The Dusk of the Gods '. Its grandeur and the manner in which the story has been written may be judged from the opening passage of ' The Rhinegold ' and the closing words of the tale :

> Long, long ago the All-Father dwelt in divine unchanging calm. Neither desire nor hope he knew, nor grief nor wrath, nor place had he nor shape ; there was naught but the primal fire.
>
> Ages of ages went by, and at last in the depths of his being awoke Desire. And the All became the Many, and the Nameless took name, and the Shapeless took shape ; and there were Earth and Sky, Day and Night, Gods and Men, Giants and Dwarfs, Desire and Hatred, Life and Death. Then said Wotan, ruler of the gods, ' By Law and by the plighted Word shall all things stand ' ; and he made covenants with all living things, yea and with the clouds of the air and the dust of the earth, that thus and thus their work and their worth should be ; and the covenants were graven in runes on the shaft of Wotan's spear.' . . .

' The Dusk of the Gods ' brings the story to an end no less impressively but on a note of hope :

> Then as they laid the body of Siegfried upon the pyre she set a torch to it and wildly the flames blazed up, and into the midst of them sprang Brynhild to her lover's side, as once through the fires he had rushed fearless to her arms. And through the smoke the sun shone with a fading glare, and ever the darkness grew and grew, but far away and aloft another conflagration glowed with answering gleam as the rejoicing flames of Loki swallowed the tall towers of Valhalla. And the Rhine swelled above its banks and broke in with a torrent of leaping waters ; above the pyre

they swept and eddied, and back into the pure bosom of the stream the Rhine-maidens bore the Nibelung's Ring.

Thus the world was ended that Wotan had made, and has filled with passion and desire, and ruled by the Spear of the Covenants. And the Spear was no more, and the Covenants no more, and Valhalla and the Gods were no more. But unconsumed in the heart of the primal flame abode eternal Love, that forever maketh all things new.

The non-publication of ' The Ring ' caused doubts in Rolleston's mind as to the ethics of accepting payment for the work he had done. The amount agreed upon with Harrap was £50, the same as for each of the three preceding books, and my father's action in the matter, which was characteristic, is related in a letter written by Harrap to my stepmother three months after Rolleston's death. The letter concerned business matters and contained this paragraph :

On looking through our records I find that we paid your husband the sum of £50 for the MS. (of ' The Ring '). £25 of this was paid at the end of 1915. I sent your husband a cheque somewhat later for the other £25, and he promptly with his usual generosity, returned it to me. However, later on, at the end of 1919 I sent him the £25 again, telling him that the worst difficulties had not eventuated and that we were quite able to pay the sum, whereupon he accepted it.

Just as the war broke out ' Tannhäuser ', Lohengrin ', and ' Parsifal ' were ready for publication in one volume without Pogány's illustrations, under the title *Sacred and Profane Love.* Publication had of course to be postponed till after the war during the course of which Arnold Bennett brought out his *Sacred and Profane Love,* in ignorance of the fact that Rolleston's printed and bound but unpublished work already bore that title. There was nothing to do therefore before the volume could eventually be put on the market but remove all the covers and bindings and alter the title—to *Three Love Tales : A Trilogy after Richard Wagner.* There are in existence, however, about half a dozen copies, of which I have one—given me by my father—with the original binding and title.

VIII

PROSE

T. W. ROLLESTON'S prose works, like his verse writings, were not very numerous, but each in its own sphere was as perfect an achievement as it could well be made. Reference has already been made to the *Life of Lessing*, but it was not only the German philosophers and writers who attracted him. My father was a Greek scholar of great eminence and was so strongly drawn to the Stoic philosophy that at the age of only twenty-four the house of Kegan Paul published his original translation from the Greek of the *Enchiridion*, or Manual, of Epictetus in a form which could be conveniently carried about. This little book penetrated to every corner of the world and was regarded by many very eminent men as the most valuable of their possessions. Walt Whitman was one of these and the *Enchiridion*, through which Whitman first made contact with Epictetus, went with him everywhere. And in far-away South Australia about nineteen years ago Sir Josiah Symon, the very deeply respected ' Grand Old Man ' of that corner of the British Empire, told me that for more years than he could remember my father's little volume had never been beyond reach of his hand and that in fact he regarded it as a book of more practical value than the Bible itself.

It would be out of place here to enter into an exposition of the philosophy of Epictetus, the crippled Phrygian slave in the household of Epaphroditus, Librarian to the Emperor Nero, who was not only nameless—Epictetus means ' bought ' or ' acquired ' and was merely a convenient designation— but who, although he was the real author of the ' Discourses ', of which the *Enchiridion* is a summary, himself wrote nothing. He lectured and his lectures were written down by Arrian, the historian of Alexander of Macedon.

Reading my father's preface to his later publication *The*

Book of Epictetus, which included the *Enchiridion*, and remembering Sir Josiah Symon's opinion, one is forced to wonder for a moment whether indeed Christianity is only 1,939 years old. So much of what Epictetus taught was not rigidly Stoical and was so full of what would now be called ' Christian principles ' that such a speculation is unavoidable. Rolleston at any rate saw the need for explaining what the teaching of Epictetus lacked as compared with the teaching of Christ. This he does in the preface referred to :

Of this (Christian) teaching Epictetus knew nothing. One can imagine his hearing it with wonder, and ultimately with delight in its profundity and truth, but he never heard it, and he never divined it. It is not essentially inconsistent with his doctrine—that doctrine needed but a little enlargement, a final touch of spiritual wisdom, to have taken it in, and thereby to have made Thought glow into Religion ; but that touch was beyond him, as it was beyond all antiquity ; it had to be given, not from any philosophic chair, but from a cross.

Allowing, however, for all this, let us not suppose that Epictetus and his teaching can ever be really superseded and laid aside. What he saw, he saw intensely, and recorded with power and fidelity. And he saw much that we would do well to see with him. He sent a piercing beam of light into the recesses of the human soul, and he discovered there the unconquerable Will, the capacity for spiritual freedom, to which in times of perplexity and discouragement troubled souls have always turned as to the sheet-anchor of their moral life. So long as fortitude and valour have any meaning in the world, so long will an iron string in the human heart respond to the words of Stoicism. Without this element Christianity itself might become, as indeed it so often is, an unstable sentimentalism, divorced from the verities of life.

Rolleston did not go so far as to say that Stoicism as taught by Epictetus was the foundation of Christianity, but he evidently saw nothing mutually repellent in the two teachings. I believe that if he himself had been asked to define his own religious belief he would have called it a combination of the practicality of Epictetus with the idealism of Christianity. If this were so and if my father did in fact live up to those two standards, which he regarded as complementary, then no one, I think, who knew him would deny that the world would be a far better place if more of its citizens should elect to be guided by the same combination of principles. Could those two virtues, toleration and charity, be better expounded or more highly extolled than in this passage from the *Enchiridion* ?

XLV. Doth any one bathe in a mighty little time ? Do not say, that he doth it ill ; but, in a mighty little time. Doth any one drink a great quantity of wine? Do not say that he doth ill; but, that he drinks a great quantity. For, unless you perfectly understand the principle (from which any one acts), how should you know if he acts ill? Thus you will not run the hazard of assenting to any appearances, but such as you fully comprehend.

This passage and many others from the ' Discourses ' and the *Enchiridion* might well be transferred to the New Testament without detracting one iota from the value of Christ's teaching. Is there indeed any essential difference between the above and St. Luke vi, verses 36 and 37 ? ' Be ye therefore merciful, as your Father also is merciful. Judge not, and ye shall not be judged ; condemn not, and ye shall not be condemned ; forgive, and ye shall be forgiven.'

T. W. Rolleston's own contribution to philosophical literature was contained in a book which, although it was very highly praised by every critic who noticed it, did not reach as wide a public as it deserved. This book, which was particularly appreciated in Germany, is called *Parallel Paths : A Study of Biology, Ethics, and Art* ; it was published by Duckworth and Company in 1908 and was reprinted in ' The Readers' Library ' in 1912.

I do not propose to write at any great length about this book ; it is one that many a man who had spent a lifetime in a purely academic and philosophical atmosphere would have considered as the crowning achievement of his life's work. It evidences an immense amount of reading and study, the possession of an analytical mind of the first order, an astounding memory, and an earnest desire to ' get at the truth of things '. For a man like T. W. Rolleston, whose life up to 1906—when he began to write *Parallel Paths*—had been concerned with such things—essentially practical matters—as organising and lecturing on industries and manufactures, piloting to success the greatest literary movement of the modern world, and planning the rescue and regeneration of his native land, to have even contemplated the writing of such a book argues courage and self-confidence of a remarkable order. But then T. W. Rolleston was that sort of man ; his brain had an infinite capacity for absorbing and retaining knowledge and, though the actual writing of *Parallel Paths* occupied little more than two years, it had been turning over in his brain and its form had been crystallising in his mind for probably more than thirty years. It was when his work with the Department of Agriculture ended in 1905, leaving no other important occupation ready to his hand, that he decided to retire to County Wicklow and, among the lovely hills and valleys and trees of that beautiful corner of Ireland, to put his philosophical ideas in order and set them down in writing.

The first portion of *Parallel Paths*, that dealing with Biology, consists in the main of an examination of the theories and arguments of many different students of natural phenomena —Paley, Darwin, Lamarck, Weismann, Haeckel, and many others—but it contains also much original thought on the subject. Like his distinguished predecessors in this field Rolleston was investigating the possibility of explaining life and the universe and its apparently inscrutable workings in chemical and mechanical terms only and to the exclusion of a Divine Being. In the pursuit of this aim the reader is led into channels of absorbing fascination, but always without arriving at any conclusion except that, in the last resort, there must exist an all-powerful Divinity. Having shown, for example, that one phenomenon or circumstance is the natural and inevitable result of some pre-existing condition, the question invariably arises as to what in turn created that condition itself ; and, having answered that question satisfactorily and found a still more remote pre-determining factor, that question must be repeated, answered, and repeated again ; in fact, to quote from *Parallel Paths* :

> There is always a ' beyond ' for the exploration of the intellect. The function of the intellect is to combine and reduce to order the experiences of sense, thus guiding us with definite aim through the bewildering wonders of life. But let us not dream that it can ever guide us to any goal or terminus. The goal is at once infinitely distant and nearer than our breath and blood. The search for it will last as long as Time.

Parallel Paths is not in any sense a technical book ; it is written in language which, though necessarily employing some terms that are not in everyday use, still makes it completely intelligible to any one with a good education. It is almost, but not quite, a book for ' popular ' reading.

The sections on Ethics and Art are of equally absorbing interest and the book concludes with a number of appendices amplifying and exemplifying some of the ethical and other questions dealt with in the body of the book. The whole three hundred pages—for this is not a lengthy publication—constitute a notable contribution to the literature of philosophy.

In a very different field from *Parallel Paths* was Rolleston's *Myths and Legends of the Celtic Race*. The former book embodied a search for truth, an exposition of facts, and a tracing of the effects on each other of a multitude of natural phenomena. In the *Myths and Legends* my father set himself the very different task of writing a history of Irish mythology, or of Celtic mythology rather, for the book deals with English, Scottish, and Welsh imaginative tales as well as with those of Ireland. The use of the word 'history' in this connection might seem rather like a contradiction in terms, but I have used it advisedly, for it would be difficult to find a national mythology that reads more like a relation of facts than does the mythology of Ireland.

The *Myths and Legends of the Celtic Race* is not a mere collection of stories of the Hans Andersen type but a practically continuous narrative dealing with the successive mythical invasions of Ireland, explaining their symbolism, and giving in some cases tables of descent of the real and imaginary Kings and Gods and demi-Gods who ruled and swayed the destinies of the country. There is nothing of the 'once-upon-a-time' atmosphere about the old Irish myths and the reader of such a book as the *Myths and Legends* cannot fail to be struck by the coherence of the whole story, by the never-varying relationship between the various titanic beings and marvellous figures that strode across the Irish mythological stage, and more especially by the accuracy with which the actual scenes of legendary and mythological events can be identified on a modern atlas. Things did not just happen 'in Ireland'; they took place in definite localities and many of them are commemorated in existing place-names. The tale of how the Shannon River got its name, the reason why Glandore Bay in County Cork is so called, the origin of Knockainey (Ainé's Hill), the story of the quaintly-named 'Haven of the Pin', and many other entrancing legends are all to be found in this fascinating textbook. So circumstantial are many of these absorbing tales that it is difficult indeed to realise that one is not reading history. At the end of Chapter V of the book—the chapter dealing with the tales of the Ultonian Cycle, which centre round the redoubtable Cuchullin— Rolleston sums up the situation thus :

Before leaving this great cycle of legendary literature let us notice what has already, perhaps, attracted the attention of some readers—the extent to which its chief characters and episodes have been commemorated in the still surviving place-names of the country.   This is true of Irish legend in general—it is especially so of the Ultonian Cycle.   Faithfully indeed, through many a century of darkness and forgetting, have these names pointed to the hidden treasures of heroic romance which the labours of our own day are now restoring to light.   The name of the little town of Ardee, as we have seen, commemorates the tragic death of Ferdia at the hand of his ' heart companion ',[1] the noblest hero of the Gael.   The ruins of Dūn Baruch, where Fergus was bidden to the treacherous feast, still look over the Waters of Moyle, across which Naisi and Deirdre sailed to their doom.   Ardnurchar, the Hill of the Sling-cast, in Westmeath, brings to mind the story of the stately monarch, the crowd of gazing women, and the crouching enemy with the deadly missile which bore the vengeance of Mesgedra.   The name of Armagh, or Ard Macha—the Hill of Macha —enshrines the memory of the Fairy Bride and her heroic sacrifice, while the grassy rampart can still be traced where the war-goddess in the earlier legend drew its outline with the pin of her brooch when she founded the Royal Fortress of Ulster.   Many pages might be filled with these instances. Perhaps no modern country has place-names so charged with legendary associations as are those of Ireland.   Poetry and myth are there still closely wedded to the very soil of the land—a fact in which there lies ready to hand an agency for education, for inspiration, of the noblest kind, if we only had the insight to see it and the art to make use of it.

The story of Deirdre and Naisi mentioned above has already been briefly related, but for the other tales the reader must turn to the *Myths and Legends* or else to my father's *The High Deeds of Finn* [2] where many of them are re-told in greater detail.

I find it difficult to leave this subject without making some comparison between the Ireland of legend and myth—and indeed the Ireland of early history—and the Ireland of to-day. It is very noticeable that at all times, real and imaginary, the people of Erin looked up to, followed, obeyed, and even rever- enced a King or Kings who were surrounded and served by an aristocracy : all the myths and legends that have been handed down, whether the tales be sad or heroic or cruel, as they sometimes were, centre round the doings of these members of a ruling caste.   This caste was generally one of

[1] Cuchullin.   [2] George G. Harrap and Company, 1910.

fighting men and brave women whose outstanding characteristic was that they were real aristocrats and their Kings were
real Kings whose commands were obeyed. They were less
Gods and Goddesses than human beings cast in moulds of
the highest nobility and endowed with superhuman attributes
both in themselves and in their magical weapons. The Irish
people of ancient times created these beings, whose exploits
must have been in most cases based on actual happenings
elaborated by keen imaginations, because the mentality and
outlook of the Celtic race needed them. The fact is that the
Irish, like their kinsfolk of Scotland and the Hebrides, are
essentially an aristocratic race ; there is no subservience
about the Irish peasant, who can be led but cannot be driven,
and the people of Erin need a King and a ruling caste every
bit as much to-day as in the days of old ; they are as necessary
to the Irish race as Admirals, Generals, and other Officers
are to Navies and Armies.

There is no place in Ireland for Socialism, for the ' every-
man-as-good-as-his-neighbour ' type of national life, which is
one reason why I at any rate regard the present régime in
Ireland as destined to be only temporary ; the words ' Irish
Republic ' seem to me mutually contradictory. This points
to one of the gravest mistakes that England has made in
dealing with the sister island—I refer to the infrequency of
Royal Visits to that country. Queen Victoria paid, I think,
only one visit to Ireland and that not till she had been sixty-
three years on the Throne ; in spite of this discourtesy,
as one might well call it, to a people who value courtesy
highly, her reception was tumultuous. So was King Edward's
when he went there a year or two later. On the former
occasion only one disloyal emblem made its appearance in
Dublin and that was a black flag flown—till it had been
removed—from the house of a lady who was largely English
—Maud Gonne.

But the Irish people need a real King and Queen, not an
absentee Monarch, and when the present phase has run its
course and the seal set on a real settlement of the Irish question
—which is at the moment merely in abeyance—by a visit
from the reigning Monarch let it be hoped that the event
will not be an isolated one but at least an annual occurrence.

Let it be remembered too that no one has a better right to

sit on an Irish Throne than a member of the House of Windsor, and that even the Coronation Chair in Westminster Abbey was made to be a Shrine for a Stone which is Irish property. This is what my father says of this matter in the *Myths and Legends* :

Tuan mac Carell says they (the Danaans) came to Ireland ' out of heaven '. This is embroidered in later traditions into a narrative telling how they sprang from four great cities, whose very names breathe of fairy-dom and romance—Falias, Gorias, Finias, and Murias. Here they learned science and craftsmanship from great sages, one of whom was enthroned in each city, and from each they brought with them a magical treasure. From Falias came the Stone called *Lia Fail*, or the Stone of Destiny, on which the High-Kings of Ireland stood when they were crowned, and which was supposed to confirm the election of a rightful monarch by roaring under him as he took his place on it. The actual stone which was so used at the inauguration of a reign did from immemorial times exist at Tara, and was sent thence to Scotland early in the sixth century for the crowning of Fergus the Great, son of Erc, who begged his brother Murtagh mac Erc, King of Ireland, for a loan of it. An ancient prophecy told that wherever this Stone was, a King of the Scotic (i.e., Irish-Milesian) race should reign. This is the famous Stone of Scone, which never came back to Ireland, but was removed to England by Edward I in 1297, and is now the Coronation Stone in Westminster Abbey. Nor has the old prophecy been falsified, since through the Stuarts and Fergus mac Erc the descent of the British Royal Family can be traced from the historic Kings of Milesian Ireland.

IX

THE END

THERE is little now to add to this record of a very full and useful life. My father was at work up to the very day of his death. After getting up on the morning of Sunday, 5 December 1920, he said he was not feeling up to the mark ; but he came down as usual and had a light breakfast. No one thought anything was seriously the matter and a little later he could have been seen in the garden, where he was tidying up and collecting odd bits of stick and twigs that had blown off the trees and which he put in a basket to be used later as kindling for the central-heating furnace ; this was a job he often did.

A little before 10 a.m. he was seen to put down the basket rather suddenly and walk back to the house in a way that suggested he was very tired. He lay down on a couch in the dining-room while my stepmother obtained a doctor. But nothing could be done ; soon afterwards he lost consciousness and he died quietly and peacefully at eleven o'clock. His heart, strained by the intensity with which he had filled his sixty-three years with work and overwhelmed by the stress of emotions evoked not only by the war but by the sad condition of his beloved Ireland, suddenly ceased work.

It was a merciful end—the sort of end he deserved ; it came as a shock to those who loved him and to his hosts of friends, who found it hard to believe that such a vital personality had been taken away at such a comparatively early age.

Many tributes were paid to him by those with and for whom he had worked. Extracts from some of these have already been used in the foregoing pages but others also merit quotation. First his life-long friend, H. B. Cotterill, in *The Times* :

I feel sure that you will allow me to add a few words to what has been said about one whose death has elicited already the expression of so much sorrow and so much affection. I have hesitated somewhat long ; but you will understand me when I say that, had it been possible—which it is not —I should have preferred to express in private to your correspondents my profound gratitude for their admiration for the character, and of the brilliant intellectual gifts of one who, for more than forty years, in sunshine and in shade, was for me the truest of friends—indeed, more like a brother than a friend—a frequent companion, in Germany, in Switzerland, in Ireland, and in England—a never-failing sympathiser in every literary or artistic subject that happened to interest me—a constant, for long spells almost a daily, correspondent, whose letters, however brief, always brought illumination. And in saying this I omit what was of far greater value than any merely intellectual comradeship—namely that strengthening of courage and faith which one gains by long contact with a fearless seeker after truth, and that exaltation of soul that one feels at possessing the intimate and affectionate friendship of such a human being.

The late Dr. Cloudesley Brereton also wrote in *The Times* :

The sudden death of T. W. Rolleston must have come as a shock to his numerous friends. It would indeed be difficult to say in which particular sphere of culture he will most be missed. He tried his hand at so many things and all he attempted he did well, often exceedingly well. In this age of ultra-specialism he showed that a man may still make himself a name in more than one branch of human activity. His remarkable versatility was broad-based on a sympathy at once intellectual and personal. He was equally at home in German literature and Indian art, in Irish literature and Irish archaeology. In fact, anything Irish appealed to him. Like his friend, ' AE ', he interested himself alike in Irish art and economics. He had also an extensive acquaintance with philosophy, science, and psychical research, together with a wide experience of editing and journalism.

But *abeunt studia in mores*, and this many-sided culture undoubtedly helped to fortify and develop a character of singular attractiveness and suavity. Some one has remarked that not only the average Englishman's house is his castle, but that he himself is more or less one. There are countersigns to be mastered, shibboleths to be exchanged before unrestricted entry is permitted. With Rolleston no passwords were necessary. One entered, so to say, an open house, and at once felt at home. There was a wonderful buoyancy—one had almost written ' boyishness '—in his attitude towards men and things. His erect and alert bearing gave no inkling of his age. One would never imagine he was over fifty, much less over sixty. With his death the saying that those the gods love die young acquires a new meaning.

What the Greeks described as εὔκολος, and the Latins, in talking of the wisdom of Laelius, as *mitis*, was probably the dominant note of his sensitive though not fastidious character. Many Irishmen are free and easy-going, but nearly all seem liable to brain-storms when politics or religion come up for discussion. Rolleston's sunny nature had no such cyclonic counterpart. It was just this ' gentleness ' in the fine old-fashioned sense of the word that endeared him so much to his friends, that type of gentleness which is the essential element of that sadly misused word—gentleman. I do not think he ever said an unkind thing, and though his wit was always *en vedette*, there was nothing of that mordant bitterness about it that one associates with Irish sallies. Considerate for others, he never spared himself, and at the beginning of the war, though over fifty-seven, he enlisted as a veteran. Later on he took an active part in the propaganda campaign. The pamphlet he wrote for neutrals on the Irish problem was a masterpiece of clarity and candour. In any enumeration of his principal achievements mention must be made of his work under his friend Horace Plunkett in Ireland, especially in reference to Irish Industries and the Irish Industries Association. Rolleston always believed that the solution of Ireland's difficulties lay in economic rather than political reform, as indeed he stated in an article in the *Nineteenth Century and After* as recently as last August. His interest in the Ireland of the past was equally strong. He was Secretary of the Irish Literary Society of London, and published several books, notably *A Treasury of Irish Poetry* in conjunction with Stopford Brooke. Indian art, again, owes him an immense debt. Most of what we know to-day of Indian art is due to the India Society, of which he was one of the foundation members and Honorary Secretary. He was a poet of no mean merit—his stanzas written at Clonmacnoise are in several anthologies—and also a great authority on German literature. The numerous reviews he contributed to *The Times Literary Supplement* displayed a rare competence of knowledge and a wide catholicity of judgment. He was in fact an admirable specimen of that curious combination that alone our British and Irish universities seem able to turn out—the combination of the gentleman and the scholar, who is neither boor nor pedant. To use the old Renaissance term—Rolleston was a complete humanist.

Alfred Perceval Graves, the famous author of 'Father O'Flynn', wrote in the *Irish Book Lover*:

I was much shocked and distressed at the cruel intelligence of the awfully sudden death of our dear friend, Rolleston. He was doubly connected with me, through my father's family on his own side, and through my mother by his first wife—she was a de Burgh. He became godfather to my son, Robert, who is now emulating his poetic and practical tastes. For, indeed, he combined the best qualities of the man of letters and the man of business in a remarkable degree. Few Irishmen have had such a fine record as his. A poet of fine finish, rising occasionally to noble inspiration as in his 'Dead at Clonmacnoise' and the 'Maeldune' poems, a delightful dealer with Irish rhythms—and those indeed of the Celtic race generally—a man of high musical and artistic tastes, and one of such versatile gifts and conversational charm to impart them to others. Altogether he was an Irishman of the ablest gifts and capacities. Personally he was equally distinguished—tall, well-proportioned, and strikingly handsome. But above all I, for one, shall value him for his absolute sincerity, as a man of letters, a politician, and, in any case, a dear relative and friend.

But perhaps the most moving tribute of all was contained in the words of the late Reverend Henry Gow, who conducted my father's funeral service at Hampstead on 9 December 1920 :

We gather here in the presence of the mystery of death to thank God for the life He gave and which He has now taken from us, and to say for a little time—Farewell !

We would bring the tribute of respect, of sorrow, and of love, not the tribute of praise. He would not have wished for praise and it is only in a very few words that I would try to express the sorrow and the love of those who knew him.

We thank God to-day for the sacred memories of him which fill our hearts. We remember the beauty of his face, the dignity of his bearing, the light and welcome of his smile. There were gentleness and affection and manly strength in all his words and looks. He was a mystic and a man of action, a poet and a thinker, a dreamer of noble dreams and a scholar, an idealist and a man of the world. We felt there was that in him which was capable of being a leader of men and of solving problems which Statesmen had found insoluble. He loved Ireland with a deep and sacred love ; he knew and shared her passion for the beautiful, her sense of the unseen, her love of liberty. He had also the Irish vein of melancholy and her gaiety of heart, her mystic visions. When he spoke of her we listened to him as to one who spoke with authority, the authority of love and the authority of knowledge. The troubles of this present time weighed heavily upon his mind and filled him with deep sympathetic pain.

We remember him as companion and friend, how generous he was, how quick to respond, how happy in the happiness of others.

We remember the beauty of his home and the sacred wonder of his love for those who were nearest and dearest to him.

He stands out in our memory as a unique and noble personality, like no other man we have known. He had a yearning for the infinite, for a perfection and beauty never wholly to be found upon this earth, united with a deep and loving appreciation of the common things of daily life. He was fastidious and yet catholic in his tastes, firm and yet tolerant in his views, brave and yet gentle in his life. He looked out into the future with a wondering and steadfast hope. He had felt to his heart's core the beauty of the world, the joy of life, the wonder of existence. No interpretation of life and death could be true for him which did not mean the eternal value of beauty and of love. Remember his words written a year ago upon ' Immortality ' : ' I am satisfied that whatever we have made, whatever we have been, even to our inmost unspoken thoughts, remains a part of the texture of the Universe. If two souls have loved each other here, that love has enriched the Universe for ever and will work there for ever. It is right that the divine secret of the grave should be impenetrable to earthly eyes. Christianity in a thousand utterances of infinite tenderness has warned us that the passion for the individual must not blind us to the claim of the Power who embraces all and who gives us the very faculty of loving. *That* remains and in saying with Dante " In His Will is our Peace " then and then only we can truly reach beyond the grave into the region where our departed are.'

Those of us who knew and loved his poems seem to hear him speak to us to-day in our sorrow words of encouragement and of hope :

> Old days, old friends, we part, we part ;
> Yet still your memory in my heart
> Lives, till the heart be dust ; and then
> Beyond this realm of Where and When,
> Something of you shall linger yet,
> And something in me not forget,
> When all the suns of earth have set.

My father had written these lines many years before in memory of his friend of the Rob Roy canoe days, Jack Humphreys. Another of his most beautiful poems will fittingly bring this record to an end :

THE SONG OF MAELDUIN

> There are veils that lift, there are bars that fall,
>   There are lights that beckon and winds that call—
>   Good-bye !
>   There are hurrying feet, and we dare not wait ;
> For the hour is on us, the hour of Fate,
>   The circling hour of the flaming Gate—
> Good-bye, good-bye, good-bye !
>
> Fair, fair they shine through the burning zone,
>   Those rainbow gleams of a world unknown—
>   Good-bye !
>   And oh, to follow, to seek, to dare,
> When step by step in the evening air
>   Floats down to meet us the cloudy stair—
> Good-bye, good-bye, good-bye !
>
> The cloudy stair of the Brig o' Dread
>   Is the dizzy path that our feet must tread—
>   Good-bye !
>   O all ye children of Nights and Days
> That gather and wonder and stand at gaze,
>   And wheeling stars in your lonely ways—
> Good-bye, good-bye, good-bye !

The music calls and the gates unclose,
Onward and upward the wild way goes—
Good-bye !
We die in the bliss of a great new birth,
O fading phantoms of pain and mirth,
O fading loves of the old green Earth,
Good-bye, good-bye, good-bye !

INDEX TO DATES

INDEX

173

Printed in Great Britain by
Butler & Tanner Ltd.,
Frome and London